WHY WE RULE!

WHY WE RULE!

1★0★1
Great Reasons to Love Our Country

ROB COHEN *and*
DAVID WOLLOCK

HarperEntertainment
An Imprint of HarperCollinsPublishers

HarperCollins books may be purchased for educational,
business, or sales promotional use. For information please write:
Special Markets Department, HarperCollins Publishers Inc.,
10 East 53rd Street, New York, NY 10022.

FIRST EDITION

Designed by Adrian Leichter

Library of Congress Cataloging-in-Publication Data
Cohen, Rob, 1969–
Why we rule! : 101 great reasons to love our country /
Rob Cohen and David Wollock.—1st ed.   p. cm.
Includes bibliographical references.   ISBN 0-06-009941-0
1. United States—Civilization—Miscellanea.   2. National characteristics,
American—Miscellanea.   3. Popular culture—United States—
Miscellanea. I. Wollock, David.   II. Title
E169.1 .C619 2002   2002190220

02 03 04 05 06 RRD 10 9 8 7 6 5 4 3 2 1

Reason #102: my mom, Esther Wollock-Wolf,
whose unconditional love and support stretches
from sea to shining sea.
—*David Wollock*

For my dad, Dr. Harry Cohen,
who always wanted to be a writer,
but instead chose to save lives.
—*Rob Cohen*

ACKNOWLEDGMENTS

This book would have not been possible without the help of Christine Roth, Stefanie Relles, and Steve Mirkin, whose encyclopedic minds allowed us to do as little work ourselves as possible. Special thanks to our agent Betsy Amster for still taking our calls throughout the years, as well as thanks to Josh Behar, April Benavides, and David Brown for believing in this book, and to Michael Shullman from Getty Images for all of his hard work.

Other fine Americans who rule:

Larry Alcorn, Jim Appleby, Matt Beckwith, Bob Bell, Meshak Blaq, Michele Botwin, Bruce Burton, Sara Chazen, Angela Cheng-Caplan, Hae Min Cho, Barbara Cohen, Heather Cohen, Curt Conner, Suzanne Craig, Sean Daniels, Ben Darby, Daniel Donnelly, Bridget Ellen, Alan Eskot, Steve Ferchaud, Tom G., Lynn Garrett, Donald Garrett, Renee Geddis, David Glaubiger, Dr. Giles Gunn, Kerry Hite, Eric Knight, Brian Kriezel, Pamela LaBarbiera, Jason Leopold, Len Levallo, Samantha Lewis @ Digital Playground, Adrian Leichter, Bill Liebowitz @ Golden Apple, Bella Lookner, Rick Mahr, Susan Mainzer, Colin Malone, Marc Mani, Mr. Marcus, Mary from Trashy Lingerie, Hayden Meyer, Andrea Molitor, Tera Patrick, Trudy Perry (and Scout), Chris Petersen and ultrapixel.com, Geoffrey Philipe, Kathleen and Bill Pierce, Zane Plsek, Kurt Reighley, Jamie & Penny Ritter, Barbara Robertson, Michelle Roche, Margaret Roth, Howie Sanders, Loni Sandoval, Dani Schimmel, George Shohet, Dr. Deborah Sills, Frank Sosa, Paul Stephan, Jeff Stolz, Nora Strick, Craig Swedin, Karen Taylor and the Jumbo's Crew, Bethany Thompson, Jen Vineyard, Frankie Villareal, the Weinbergs, Wendy Weisberg, Marv Wolf, Larry Wolfe, Qlara Wollock, and everyone else who made this book possible.

INTRO

God bless America!

In a scant 226 years of existence, we've managed to cram thousands of years' worth of history, innovation, and adventure into our country. Although they *did* invent the toga and the orgy, the Greeks and Romans ain't got nothing on us. Yeah, we've got our problems, but when you look at the big picture—the big, global picture—we've done a hell of a lot in a short span of time.

Our country has given rise to the modern world's greatest thinkers, tinkerers, inventors, artists, heroes, performers, players, and pundits. We didn't come up with everything, but dammit if we don't always manage to build a better mousetrap, and we always have the most fun doing it. No, not everybody loves us, but they definitely want to party with us.

Face it: there's no country on earth where you'd rather be.

America is more than just a place. It's an idea—it's the embodiment of the world's hopes, dreams, and aspirations. We're the great melting pot, a crossbred nation of mutts, living in a land where we can make our own decisions, pull ourselves up by our own bootstraps, and chart our own destinies. We have roots in every nation on the planet, bound and bonded by one common idea: freedom.

Some of the freedoms we exercised while writing this book include irreverence, naughty language, stupidity, and opinion. If nothing else, *Why We Rule!* proves that in America, any two boneheads can write a book (or two—see our first tome, *Etiquette for Outlaws*). You'll agree resoundingly with some of our reasons, disagree with others, and wonder if we were on crack when we came up with a few of them.

Hey, you're entitled; it's a free country.

Which brings us to our methodology in determining what made the cut for our top 101 reasons to love America. After long, late nights of intense scientific, historical, and existential examinations of what makes us tick (along with a fair amount of cheap beer), we came up with what *we* thought best represented the U.S. of A., from "Freedom" to "Frivolity." These 101 reasons aren't listed in any strict order or ranking—if they were, it would suggest that we believe the invention of boob implants was more monumental than landing on the moon. Then again . . .

In some instances, we chose big, overarching, patriotic concepts such as "Entrepreneurial Spirit" to illustrate our country's greatness. Other times, we chose an iconic person or institution that we felt made some important statement about America—the Statue of Liberty, Martin Luther King Jr., Elvis, Hugh Hefner, to name a few. Many of these reasons are reinforced or "supersized" by additional, encyclopedic highlights and lists.

What's that? We forgot to include O-Town in our list of the greatest bands of all time, or failed to mention your favorite Spam recipe? Then get off your La-Z-Boy and go write your own damn book! In this land of ours, you're allowed, even if you don't have a helluva lot to say (see Reason #84).

The important thing to remember is that no single reason makes this country great. What we discovered, during our foray into American McHistory, is that what really, *truly* kicks ass about the United States is that it's filled with Americans. Americans of every race, creed, color, and religion. Americans with varied tastes in food, entertainment, politics, and vices. This book isn't just about our country. It's about realizing who we are—who *you* are. *Why We Rule!* is a chance for you to remember what you love about this country—whether it's your freedom of speech, or your fridge full of beer.

So crack open an ice-cold Bud (or blaze up a fat juicy chronic bud), pull up a chair (or grab this book on your next trip to the can), get pumped up with pride, and learn a thing or two about this great nation of ours.

Say it loud, say it proud: *We Rule!*

FREEDOM

Freedom isn't just another word for nothing left to lose; it's what this whole damn country's about. It's what makes us great—and differentiates us from the pack. In 1776, we told the British to piss off, we'll do it ourselves. And for the last two-hundred-plus years, not only have we continued to do it ourselves, we've evolved from a band of ragtag insurgents in funny-looking hats into the global superpower.

We have the freedom to do basically anything we want, as long as it doesn't mess with anyone else's lifestyle or inalienable rights. In other words, you can say, "Screw you, Mr. President!" (which would probably get you killed in some countries). We also have the freedom to buy smutty mags in the market and beer on Sunday, honk at hot chicks, and generally make asses out of ourselves anytime we see fit.

THE CONSTITUTION

It's flexible, wise, often imitated, but never duplicated. It's an illustration of mighty fine penmanship. And it made for a pretty peppy "Schoolhouse Rock" tune.

The Constitution establishes the separation of powers—Congress, the Supreme Court, and the Prez—so that no one person can grab all the power and fuck our shit up. It outlines the basic structure of America's ideals and, even better, how to implement them.

The coolest thing about our Constitution is that it's a living document, with checks, balances, and procedures for amendment built right into its very fabric. Yup, this bad boy has been working for 226 years. Like Dick Clark, it's ageless and always in tune with the times. Hell, we can't confirm it, but Dick might've even been there for the signing.

More Documents That Rule!

THE DECLARATION OF INDEPENDENCE

Written by Thomas Jefferson, and passed by the Continental Congress on July 4, 1776, this is the document that served notice to King George of England that his services were no longer required, thank you very much. Here's the really famous quote that we had to learn in high school: "We hold these Truths to be self-evident, that all Men are created equal, that they are endowed by their Creator with certain inalienable Rights, that among these are Life, Liberty, and the Pursuit of Happiness." Hard-core stuff to say to a not-so-very-nice king. These guys had balls.

THE BILL OF RIGHTS

The sister document to the Constitution, the Bill of Rights (really the first 10 amendments to the Constitution) lists a bunch of rights guaranteed to all our peeps: 1) freedom of speech, press, & religion; 2) the right to bear arms; 3) the right to trial and the right not to self-incriminate; 4) the right to a speedy trial; 5) the right to trial by jury; 6) the right against cruel and unusual punishment; and a few others. Subsequent amendments have abolished slavery, given women the right to vote, and put a cap on the amount of terms a President is allowed to serve. The twenty-first amendment repealed the eighteenth, which called for Prohibition. What the hell were they thinking?!

VARIETY

As the global epicenter for pop music and movies, it only figures we'd have the most renowned trade rags for those industries: *Billboard*, the *Hollywood Reporter*, and, of course, the bible of the entertainment industry, *Daily Variety*. Established in 1905 for showbiz—back then, theater, vaudeville, and nickelodeons—*Variety* is the numero uno source for news-at-a-glance for entertainment execs worldwide. Offering everything from hard business facts to updates on titillating scandals to concert reviews, it's famous for its ultra-clever headlines ("Hix Nix Stix Pix") and for inventing its own slick, abbreviated language ("Gotham," "DJ," "chopsocky"). We think this rag is just boffo!

Signers of the Declaration of Independence:

Adams, John (MA)

Adams, Samuel (MA)

Bartlett, Josiah (NH)

Braxton, Carter (VA)

Chase, Samuel (MD)

Clark, Abraham (NJ)

Clymer, George (PA)

Ellery, William (RI)

Floyd, William (NY)

Franklin, Benjamin (PA)

Gerry, Elbridge (MA)

Gwinnett, Button (GA)

Hall, Lyman (GA)

Hancock, John (MA)

Harrison, Benjamin (VA)

Hart, John (NJ)

Hewes, Joseph (NC)

Heyward, Thos. Jr. (SC)

Hooper, William (NC)

Hopkins, Stephen (RI)

Hopkinson, Francis (NJ)

Huntington, Samuel (CT)

Jefferson, Thomas (VA)

Lee, Francis Lightfoot (VA)

Signers of the Declaration of Independence:

Lee, Richard Henry (VA)

Lewis, Francis (NY)

Livingston, Philip (NY)

Lynch, Thomas Jr. (SC)

McKean, Thomas (DE)

Middleton, Arthur (SC)

Morris, Lewis (NY)

Morris, Robert (PA)

Morton, John (PA)

Nelson, Thos. Jr. (VA)

Paca, William (MD)

Paine, Robert Treat (MA)

Penn, John (NC)

Read, George (DE)

Rodney, Caesar (DE)

Ross, George (PA)

Rush, Benjamin (PA)

Rutledge, Edward (SC)

Sherman, Roger (CT)

Smith, James (PA)

Stockton, Richard (NJ)

Stone, Thomas (MD)

Taylor, George (PA)

Thornton, Matthew (NH)

Walton, George (GA)

Whipple, William (NH)

Williams, William (CT)

Wilson, James (PA)

Witherspoon, John (NJ)

Wolcott, Oliver (CT)

Wythe, George (VA)

APPLE PIE

Mock our culinary prowess if you must, but you certainly won't starve here. America has tons of great things to stuff your face with, from Tater Tots to California cuisine.

Of course, when it comes to American victuals, nothing rules quite as much as hot apple pie. It's the ultimate comfort food! Flip the page for a quick recipe. If it's too hard, just buy a premade version at the supermarket, another great American convenience!

RECIPE FOR APPLE PIE:

Go buy the crust—making it is a pain.

FILLING:
8 cups apples, peeled, cored, and cut into eighths
2 tablespoons lemon juice
1 cup sugar
$\frac{1}{4}$ teaspoon cinnamon
$\frac{1}{8}$ teaspoon salt
2 tablespoons flour
2 tablespoons butter, cold

Put apples in large bowl and pour lemon juice over them. In another bowl, mix dry ingredients and then add to the apples. Take your ready-made crust, and roll out one of the dough halves to an $\frac{1}{8}$-inch thickness. Lay into pie pan with a little bit overlapping the sides. Put apple mixture into pie shell, mounding it higher in the center. Cut cold butter into $\frac{1}{2}$-inch cubes and place on top of the apples. Moisten outer edge of bottom crust with water, place top crust on pie, and press down.

Preheat oven to 475 degrees F. When ready to put pie in oven, turn temperature down to 450 degrees F, and bake on lower rack until it starts to brown (around 15 minutes). Turn oven down to 375 degrees and bake approximately 1 to 1 $\frac{1}{4}$ hours.

Prep Time: 30 minutes
Cook Time: 1 hour 30 minutes

American Foods That Rule!

HOT DOGS

While the United States didn't invent the idea of sticking a sausage in a bun, the name "hot dog" is uniquely American, and thus most people assume we made the whole idea up to begin with! So where did the moniker come from? Well, let's just say someone read about it in the newspaper. In 1906, a Hearst cartoonist by the name of Tad Dorgan was catching a baseball game in New York when he heard a vender selling his frankfurters using the phrase, "Get your red-hot dachshund sausages!" Tad thought it was the funniest thing he ever heard—and immortalized the event with a cartoon in the paper of a real dog smeared with mustard on a bun, with the caption, "Get your hot dogs!" Ahh, history.

CRACKER JACK

This crunchy American classic was created by German immigrant F. W. Rueckheim in 1871, but gained its first national exposure at the 1893 Chicago World's fair as "Candied Popcorn With Peanuts." A big success, Rueckheim renamed his snack, the Cracker Jack, and by 1899 it was available in a "snack-sized" box. In 1913, CJ kicked things up a notch when they introduced their first prize. Ever since, kids around the world have enjoyed surprise goodies like decoder rings, charms, temporary tattoos, and the occasional mini Etch-A-Sketch. Cracker Jack really took off after it was immortalized in "Take Me out to the Ball Game," which recommended purchasing a box along with some peanuts.

PEANUT BUTTER

Originally invented in 1890 by a St. Louis doctor as a way for his patients to easily digest high-protein food, peanut butter became an instant hit, and by 1914 there were already several dozen brands to choose from. Today, there's nothing easier to make and eat than a PB&J. You don't have to worry about refrigeration, it's got lots of protein, and it goes great with a glass of milk or a cup of joe. According to stats, by the age of eighteen the average American child will eat over 1,500 peanut butter sandwiches. More recently, the PB&J has been re-immortalized in a famous "Got Milk" spot. Have one today! Just don't plan on whistling.

Even More Classic American Foods That Rule . . .

Anything made with pumpkin

Banana split

Big Mac

Boston baked beans

Buffalo wings

California cuisine

California roll

Campbell's chicken noodle soup

Chicago deep-dish pizza

Chicken à la King

Chili

Cobb salad

Crab cakes

Deviled eggs

Devil's food cake

Fondu

Frozen foods

Granola

Grits

Hash

Jell-O

Ketchup

Even More Classic American Foods That Rule...

Lemonade

Mac and cheese

Manhattan clam chowder

Meat loaf

Minute Rice

Nachos

Onion dip

Oysters Rockefeller

Pancakes

Philly cheese steak

Pop-Tarts

Popcorn

Ranch dressing

The Reuben

Rice-A-Roni

Roasted marshmallows

Snickers

Spam

Tuna casserole

TV dinners

Twinkies

American Foods That Rule!

POTATO CHIPS

Whether you like Lay's, Pringles, or that fancy gourmet shit, every time you crunch into a chip, you can thank Native American George Crum. George was a chef at a hoity-toity resort in Saratoga Springs, New York, where they served french fried potatoes. In 1853, a diner whined that George's fries were cut too thick. George diced up a thinner batch, but the diner sent 'em back again. Ticked off, George sliced them paper thin, hoping to piss off Mr. Finicky. Instead, his ultra-crispy snack was a hit, becoming a signature house dish. Later, chips were packaged and sold throughout New England. The advent of the mechanical potato peeler in the 1920s transformed the novelty food into a mainstream snack. And boy, do Americans love 'em, mowing through an astounding 1,969,953,342 pounds of chips a year! God only knows how much dip we use.

TABASCO SAUCE

We didn't invent ketchup, mustard, or A.1., but Tabasco hot sauce is all us. New Orleans banker Edmund McIlhenny fled his plantation during the Civil War, and returned to find his mansion and farmland all but destroyed. The only thing left was a crop of capsicum hot peppers. He turned his misfortune into a jackpot by mixing the chopped peppers with vinegar and salt and letting the sauce sit around in wood barrels. In a few years, he was selling thousands of bottles of his Cajun Tabasco for a buck each. Today, the McIlhenny Co. sticks to Ed's original recipe, selling 50 million bottles of Tabasco in the United States alone, and distributing to over 100 countries. Heck, some people are so addicted to the spicy stuff that they carry little bottles of Tabasco with them, lest they be caught at a restaurant without it.

American Foods That Rule!

CHOCOLATE CHIP COOKIES

The Romans came up with cookies, the Aztecs get the credit for cocoa powder, and a British confection company came up with the first solid eating chocolate. But it was Ruth Wakefield, proprietor of the Toll House Inn in Massachusetts, who first chopped up Nestlé chocolate bars and sprinkled the bits in her butter cookies. Toll House cookies became a national craze. Nestlé printed Ruth's recipe on the wrappers of their chocolate bars, and in exchange gave her a lifetime supply of chocolate. In addition to the chocolate chip cookie, we also came up with the popular phrase "Toss your cookies."

FUN FACTS

Mayo Madness!

The French invented "Mahonnaise," a delicate haute condiment reserved for gourmands. But in 1912, the owner of a Manhattan deli democratized the snooty sauce by premixing it and selling it in glass jars. Mayo quickly became a favorite among BLT and hamburger lovers everywhere.

INVENTORS

From the Post-it to the Internet, from Teflon to toilet paper, the famous line that we're always trying to "build a better mousetrap" is truly the mantra of amateur and professional inventors alike. Inventors in the United States register in the neighborhood of 100,000 new patents a year.

The reason?

Hand in hand with the American dream and entrepreneurial spirit is the quest to make something no one else has. Some brainchildren are brilliant, some are fun, and hey, others are quite silly. Bottom line: between freedom and capitalism is your God-given right to come up with new ideas and get paid for them.

Great American Inventors

THOMAS ALVA EDISON

With over a thousand patents to his name, Thomas Alva Edison was one prolific mo-fo. Born in Ohio, Edison worked as a telegraph operator and was known to take a few catnaps on the job—since he was working all night on other stuff. Edison's invention of the incandescent electric lightbulb alone deserves him everlasting fame, but he didn't stop there! Big Tom also invented movie cameras and phonographs, and lent a hand in developing the carbon transmitter, which helped Bell invent the telephone. Bet you didn't know that Edison also fancied himself a movie producer, lensing *The Great Train Robbery* in 1903 and the first *Frankenstein* movie in 1910.

ALEXANDER GRAHAM BELL

Born in Edinburgh, Scotland, Bell came to the United States in 1871, where he taught the deaf and mute. In 1874, while working on the development of a multiple telegraph machine, he came up with the idea for the telephone. Thought Bell, "What's the fastest way to order some takeout Chinese?" Okay, maybe not, but he did come up with the idea, inventing the first telephone in 1876. The rest is history: cell phones, fax machines, incessant telemarketers, it's all Bell's fault. Along with the telephone, Bell was also one of the founders of the National Geographic Society and the journal *Science*.

FRANK ZAPPA

Founder of the band the Mothers of Invention, Zappa and his music have never been truly understood by the masses. On the other hand, his music was cited (along with the Velvet Underground) as inspiring Vaclav Havel's "Velvet Revolution" in Czechoslovakia, which freed the country from Communism. Ultimately Zappa was appointed "Special Ambassador to the West on Trade, Culture and Tourism" for that country, and was treated like a national hero. Zappa released a ton of albums that most people have never heard of. His biggest hit song, "Valley Girl," featured a wonderfully stirring, spoken word piece from daughter Moon Unit.

American Inventions That Rule . . .

Airplane

Aluminum foil

AM radio

Animation

Antiperspirant

Automation

Band-Aid

Barbed wire

Blender

Brown paper bag

Calculator

Can opener

Chap Stick

Chewing gum

Copy machine

Crossword puzzle

Diet soda

Dishwasher

Disposable paper cup

Dr. Scholl's foot products

Electric blanket

Electric motor

Express delivery service

Electric sewing machine

Electric shaver

Flip-flops

FM radio

American Inventions That Rule...

Frisbee

Frozen orange juice

Gas-powered motor

Graphite

Hair dryer

Ice-making machine

Kerosene

Kleenex

Lightbulb

Linoleum

Microwave oven

Mimeograph

Monopoly

Nylon

Pacemaker

Pantyhose

Phonograph

Plastic

Polaroid camera

Prefabricated home

Pull-tab aluminum can

Pyrex

Richter scale

Rockets

Rubber hose

Safety elevator

Safety pin

Shorthand

Shopping carts

Silly Putty

S.O.S. pad

Steel wool

Suntan lotion

Teflon

Telegraph

Toaster

Toilet paper

Tractor

Transistors

Tuxedos

Valium

Vaseline

Vicks VapoRub

Walkie-talkie

Winchester rifle

X-ray machine

Yale lock

Zippers

UNCLE SAM

Was he a real dude . . . or not?

Though he wasn't an uncle of ours, Uncle Sam, decked out in his well-known stars-and-stripes suit and top hat, was actually based on a guy named Samuel Wilson from Massachusetts.

Sam fought in the American Revolution and helped Paul Revere warn folks that the British were coming. Later, he opened up a meat-packing company, supplying food for the troops in the War of 1812. He stamped "U.S." (for United States) on the boxes of rations. One day an employee at the plant was asked what the U.S. on the boxes stood for. Talking out of his ass, he said "Uncle Sam," referring to his boss. The name just stuck.

Eventually, illustrations of the legendary Uncle Sam began appearing in papers. At first clean-shaven, he grew a beard (a tribute to President Lincoln), and his attire steadily grew more patriotic. The Uncle Sam we know today was finally introduced on World War I army recruitment posters.

The personification of democracy, Sam lives on in everything from hot dog commercials to men on stilts hawking used cars at Fourth of July blowout sales.

OTHER ICONIC AMERICANS BASED ON REAL PEOPLE...

Johnny Appleseed, Uncle Ben, Marie Callender, the Coppertone Kid, the Gerber Baby.

FUN FACTS

 *We'll Take 'Em!*

Here's a list of famous Americans not born in the United States:

MADELEINE ALBRIGHT
(Czechoslovakia, Secretary of State)

CHARLES ATLAS *(Italy, body builder)*

MIKHAIL BARYSHNIKOV
(USSR, dancer)

IRVING BERLIN *(Russia, composer)*

FRANK CAPRA *(Italy, director)*

CLAUDETTE COLBERT
(France, actress)

XAVIER CUGAT *(Spain, musician)*

ALBERT EINSTEIN *(Germany, physicist)*

FATHER FLANAGAN
(Ireland, founded Boys Town)

FELIX FRANKFURTER
(Austria, Supreme Court justice)

KAHLIL GIBRAN *(Lebanon, writer)*

BOB HOPE
(England, you know who he is)

AL JOLSON *(Lithuania, jazz singer)*

ELIA KAZAN *(Turkey, film director)*

PEPE LEPEW *(France, skunk)*

BELA LUGOSI *(Hungary, Dracula)*

MARY PICKFORD *(Canada, actress)*

KNUTE ROCKNE
(Norway, All-American)

EDWARD G. ROBINSON
(Romania, actor)

GENE SIMMONS *(Israel, guy from Kiss)*

MR. SPOCK *(Vulcan, science officer)*

LEE STRASBERG
(Austria, acting teacher)

LEVI STRAUSS *(Germany, pants guy)*

BARON VON TRAPP
(Austria, Sound of Music guy)

RUDOLPH VALENTINO *(Italy, actor)*

PRESIDENTS

After the whole King George thing, the idea of America being ruled by a monarchy just seemed ludicrous to our Founding Fathers. Who needs a bizarre, blood-related egomaniac to muck up our affairs when we can democratically elect someone of our own choosing to muck up our affairs!

The Constitution spells out some basic qualifications—you have to be at least 35 years old, a native-born citizen of the United States, and not have a felonious background—but the rest of it is left to us. The Constitution also spells out a basic job description, and establishes a balance of power between the President and the other branches of government, to make sure than no one person or group is in charge.

We've had our great Presidents and our lame ones, but the key is that there's none of that Divine Right crap. Each Chief Exec is *of* the people, *for* the people, elected *by* the people, and his shit stinks just like everybody else's.

The Names of All 43 Chief Execs and Their Second Bananas...

1   George Washington/John Adams

2. John Adams/Thomas Jefferson

3. Thomas Jefferson/
    Aaron Burr, George Clinton

4. James Madison/George Clinton,
    Elbridge Gerry

5. James Monroe/Daniel D. Tompkins

6. John Quincy Adams/John C. Calhoun

7. Andrew Jackson/John C. Calhoun,
    Martin Van Buren

8. Martin Van Buren/
    Richard M. Johnson

9. William Henry Harrison/John Tyler

10. John Tyler/None

11. James Polk/George M. Dallas

12. Zachary Taylor/Millard Fillmore

13. Millard Fillmore/None

14. Franklin Pierce/William R. King

15. James Buchanan/John C.
    Breckinridge

16. Abraham Lincoln/Hannibal Hamlin,
    Andrew Johnson

17. Andrew Johnson/None

18. Ulysses S. Grant/Schuyler Colfax,
    Henry Wilson

19. Rutherford B. Hayes/William A.
    Wheeler

20. James A. Garfield/Chester A. Arthur

21. Chester A. Arthur/None

22. Grover Cleveland/Thomas Hendricks

Great American Presidents

GEORGE WASHINGTON

He was first in war, first in peace, and first in the hearts of his countrymen. This Founding Father led the colonial armies to victory against the British. He turned down becoming "the American King," but was our first elected President and set the tone for all future Presidents. He coined the name "Mr. President" as how the President should be addressed. He also wore a funny wig and had wooden choppers. Though he didn't really cut down a cherry tree, it's still a good story and the moral—you should always tell the truth—still stands. By the way, he did not die of syphilis. That story is a load of crap.

THOMAS JEFFERSON

Our first redheaded President, Jefferson's accomplishments are immeasurable. He was a member of the second Continental Congress; drafted the Declaration of Independence; argued for and got a bill signed establishing the separation of church and state; and consulted on the drafting of the Constitution and Bill of Rights. Elected the 3rd U.S. Prez by one vote over Aaron Burr, he was responsible for the Louisiana Purchase from France. After the death of his wife, TJ shacked up with his slave Sally Hemmings on the QT and fathered six kids with her. Actually, we don't know if it was really on the QT at the time, but we certainly didn't learn about it in high school.

Great American Presidents

ALEXANDER HAMILTON

Okay, so he was never elected President, but we figured since he's on the $10 bill and Ulysses S. Grant was a drunk, we'd give it up for Hamilton. Born in 1757 and educated at King's College (now Columbia University), he commanded an infantry regiment in the battle of Yorktown and wrote many of the *Federalist Papers*. Hamilton is most noteworthy, however, for being the first U.S. Secretary of the Treasury, where he established a national bank and credit system. Hamilton is also well known for being the tie-breaking vote who gave Thomas Jefferson the Presidency over Aaron Burr. Burr later shot Hamilton in a duel because he was pissed.

FUN FACTS

The Father of Invention!

While he was Secretary of State, Thomas Jefferson, an inventor and scientist himself, created the Patent Office (which he called the "Board of Arts"). The system he created for patents is very similar to the one we use today: by setting reasonable time limits on patents, we foster innovation without making new inventions inaccessible to the people. Of the sixty-seven patents Jefferson granted, one was to Eli Whitney for the cotton gin!

The Names of All 43 Chief Execs and Their Second Bananas...

23. Benjamin Harrison/Levi P. Morton

24. Grover Cleveland/
Adlai E. Stevenson

25. William McKinley/Garret A. Hobart,
Teddy Roosevelt

26. Teddy Roosevelt/
Charles W. Fairbanks

27. William Howard Taft/
James S. Sherman

28. Woodrow Wilson/
Thomas R. Marshall

29. Warren G. Harding/Calvin Coolidge

30. Calvin Coolidge/Charles G. Dawes

31. Herbert Hoover/Charles Curtis

32. Franklin D. Roosevelt/
John N. Garner, Henry A. Wallace,
Harry S. Truman

33. Harry S. Truman/Alben W. Barkley

34. Dwight D. Eisenhower/
Richard M. Nixon

35. John F. Kennedy/Lyndon B. Johnson

36. Lyndon B. Johnson/
Hubert Humphrey

37. Richard Nixon/Spiro T. Agnew,
Gerald R. Ford

38. Gerald R. Ford/Nelson Rockefeller

39. Jimmy Carter/Walter Mondale

40. Ronald Reagan/George Bush

41. George Bush/Dan Quayle

42. Bill Clinton/Al Gore

43. George W. Bush/Dick Cheney

Great American Presidents

ABRAHAM LINCOLN

Americans really have to rethink our priorities when you consider that in today's media-image-driven society, Honest Abe would never be elected to office. Born in a Kentucky log cabin and schooled at home, he was tall, awkward, liked big hats, and was afflicted with long-term medical problems. Yet he was the greatest Chief Executive we've ever had. Lincoln freed the slaves and kept the Union together, while his rockin' Gettysburg Address stands as the greatest speech given by a President. Said Abe: "As I would not be a slave, so I would not be a master. This expresses my idea of democracy." Lincoln was assassinated by a bad actor who gave new meaning to the phrase "Break a leg."

TEDDY ROOSEVELT

"Speak softly and carry a big stick" has always been our motto, too, but Teddy had something else in mind when he said it. A hero of the Spanish-American War (he was a Rough Rider) and former governor of New York, Roosevelt was a loudmouth, and got the Vice President nod from William McKinley largely to keep him quiet in the dummy slot. But when McKinley was assassinated in 1901, that Second Fiddle with the high, funny voice ended up with his face on Mt. Rushmore. Roosevelt's accomplishments include setting up antitrust, antimonopoly, and pro-workers' rights laws; building the Panama Canal; and winning the Nobel prize for mediating the Russo-Japanese War. Oh, and the teddy bear was named after him.

FRANKLIN ROOSEVELT

Our only four-term President (they changed the rules in 1951), FDR got us through the Great Depression and kept the nation on a steady course through most of World War II. Despite having polio and being largely confined to a wheelchair, he

Great American Presidents

remained larger than life to a constituency who loved him. In addition to his New Deal, he set up Social Security and the idea of unemployment insurance. FDR beat out Thomas Dewey in 1944 to win his fourth term. Sadly, he died in office the next year. We should also mention his wife, Eleanor. FDR's intellectual equal, she set the standard for presidential wives.

JOHN F. KENNEDY

Smart, good-looking, an eloquent speaker and great on television, John F. Kennedy was the first President born in the twentieth century and gave it its archetypal leader. The son of a bootlegger, he served in the navy in World War II (PT-109), and was elected to the Congress and then the Senate. In 1960 he beat out then-V.P. Dick Nixon to become the 35th Prez. His accomplishments include standing up to those damn Russkies during the Cuban Missile Crisis, signing the Limited Test Ban Treaty, establishing the Peace Corps...and banging Marilyn Monroe. Almost forty years later, nobody's quite sure who *really* killed JFK—Oswald, the Mob, the CIA?—making him the patron saint of conspiracy theories, with more books published about him than any other President.

RONALD REAGAN

The Gipper. Our oldest elected President, Ronald Reagan is an American original. Born in 1911, he became a sportscaster in 1937 and then moved to Hollywood, where he was an actor in bad movies for more than twenty-five years. Though he didn't get the role of Rick in *Casablanca*, Reagan was in several *Bedtime for Bonzo* installments. Elected head of the Screen Actors Guild six times, he jumped into real politics as governor of California in 1966. Elected President in 1980, Reagan championed cutting taxes and ultimately brought down the Soviet Union without firing a shot (he spent them into the ground). He was also a man of great quips. Upon being shot by would-be assassin John Hinkley, Reagan told his wife, "Honey, I forgot to duck."

BILL CLINTON

On any given day, you could find his lips wrapped around his beloved horn, or someone else's lips wrapped around his beloved horn. Hmm. Nevertheless, we still love this guy! The only modern President to be impeached? Who cares. He balanced the budget and sent stocks through the roof. And if our wallets feel fat, frankly, we as Americans don't care where he puts his cigar. Clinton, with all of his faults, gave us our longest period of sustained economic growth. He won his second term over Bob Dole handily, and probably would have won a third term if he was allowed. Hell, we'd still vote for him!

SAM ADAMS

Though America was founded on hard work and mainly Puritan princi-
ples, having a few cold ones at the end of the day sure made our work
easier. Our forefathers liked their suds so much that instead of waiting
for their first shipment from England, they brewed it themselves in
1587 in Virginia using corn. In 1612, Adrian Block and Hans Chris-
tiansen opened the first American brewery in Manhattan. And while
they couldn't just go buy a home-brewing kit at Williams-Sonoma, early
Americans like George Washington made their own beer.

Another Founding Father/beer lover was Samuel Adams, leader of the
Boston Tea Party, one of the Sons of Liberty (the dudes who cried "no tax-
ation without representation"), and signer of the Declaration of Independence. In addition to being a patriot, Sam was also a master brewer. Today
his beer is still enjoyed nationwide, and has been selected four times by
the American Association of Brewers as the best domestically made beer.

In addition to Sam Adams, America makes a ton of other good beers,
from microbrews like Sierra Nevada to macrobrews like Bud and Miller.
And while we can't confirm this, we're fairly sure the beer-bong and "keg-
gers" are both products of American ingenuity.

FUN FACTS

Oh Say Can You Drink!

Our national anthem, "The Star-Spangled Banner," was written to the tune of a drinking song!

BLOW JOBS

Get your mind out of the gutter, you perv! We're not talking about THAT. Oral pleasuring was practiced long before our nation came into existence.

But the Blow Job cocktail was definitely a product of American mixology, as were the Mai Tai, Hurricane, Mint Julep, Sex on the Beach, Fuzzy Navel, Slippery Nipple, and any number of other sweet, silly, foofy drinks guaranteed to give you a hangover. But hey, they sure are fun to order.

RECIPE FOR A GOOD BJ ...

In a shot glass, mix 1 part Kahlua, 1 part Bailey's. Top with whipped cream. Without using hands, clench glass with mouth, tilt head back, suck, and swallow. (Variations include Banana Liqueur, Irish Cream, Grand Marnier, and Crème de Banana.)

More Drinks That Rule!

BOURBON

Okay, we've got nothing bad to say about Scotch, but we should be damned proud of our own local hooch, bourbon. Made from good ol' U.S. corn, it was first distilled by a Baptist minister named Elijah Craig in Kentucky. Hallelujah! We believe! Bourbon is known worldwide under the brand names of Jim Beam, Old Grand-Dad, and Wild Turkey. Enjoy it straight, or over ice. If you want to get fancy—and it's a nice hot day—try a mint julep. Just take some mint and a simple syrup of water and sugar, add some bourbon, and serve over lotsa crushed ice.

THE MARTINI

Whether it was actually invented in San Francisco or New York, you can't go wrong with a martini. It's simple. It's elegant. It's classic Americana. And boy, can it get you hammered in a hurry! This is how you make 'em:

> 2 oz of good gin or vodka
> A "stare" of dry vermouth
> 2-3 good olives

Pour ice and ice water into a clean martini glass and let it chill while you mix the other stuff. Take a shaker, add ice and a bit of dry vermouth. Shake that up a bit, then spill the vermouth into the sink... now add your gin/vodka. Shake. Spill out the water from the glass, replace with martini, add olives... and cheers!

NAPA VALLEY WINES

Thomas Jefferson first brought French wine grapes to the States, and while we'd like to say that Americans have been making great wine ever since, the truth is that Prohibition literally poured years of hard work down the drain. But thanks to California's Napa Valley, in less than four score years, our local grape juice has made a monster comeback. Settled in the late 1800s by French, German, and Italian immigrants, Napa had the perfect climate for grapes to do their thing. At first the region's wineries churned out crappy jug wine by the gallon. It wasn't until Robert Mondavi came along that our vino started to get respect... nay, acclaim. Today, Napa wines rank right up there with Europe's best vintages.

Even More Fun American Drinks...

Alabama Sheriff

Albino Meltdown

Alarm Clock

Americano

Amy's Lover

B-52

Ball 'n' Chain

Beer Buster

Blizzard

Brass Monkey

Burnt Surfer

Burp 'n' Squirt

Cactus Colada

Cakewalk

Calamity Jane

Climax

Coke & Dagger

Depth Charge

Dogfight

D-Train

Dumb Blonde

Empire

Earthquake

Even More Fun American Drinks . . .

Fallen Angel

Fizzbomb

Goldfinger

Greenback

Headless Horseman

Horny Monkey

Igloo Melter

Jock's Strap

Juke & Jolt

Kentucky Cooler

Kiss of Death

Lab Experiment

Mai Tai

Midnight Cocktail

Melon Ball

Nail in the Coffin

Orange Blossom

Pacemaker

Park Avenue

Poop Deck

Quick Fix

Rusty Nail

Santa Fe

Tennessee Express

Torpedo

Vampire Kiss

Volcano Cooler

Wasp Attack

Yak's Milk

Zombie

HELEN KELLER

Anytime you think you've got it tough and the deck is stacked against you, stop whining like a little bitch, and think of the heroic life of Helen Keller.

Born your basic normal kid in 1880, Keller caught a bad fever as a baby and came close to dying. Though she survived, she was left blind and deaf. But in America, when you have lemons you make lemonade. Honing her other senses, she could recognize faces simply by touching them. This wasn't enough for a smart cookie like Helen, and her frustration with her disability manifested itself with fits of rage. Enter Anne Sullivan, a private tutor who had lost her sight, only to regain it later. Recognizing that Helen's tantrums came from her inability to communicate, Sullivan taught her to read and write Braille, and to read lips by touch.

Keller went on to write *The Story of My Life*, and with the dough she made, she bought a house. Among other accomplishments, she lectured across America and Europe, eventually becoming a suffragette. Not impressed? What the hell have *you* done with your life?

FREEDOM OF RELIGION

In America, you have the right to worship anything you like, whether it's at the church down the block or at the Universal Church of Elvis.

When the Pilgrims took that trip on the *Mayflower,* it wasn't a pleasure cruise. They braved scurvy, rats, lice, and other icky stuff to escape religious persecution. Hence the fact that we have no state-sponsored religion, and we have a nifty principle called "the separation of church and state." What this means is that you can worship whoever, whatever, and however you want, as long as it does not infringe upon the rights of others.

Because of this freedom, America has a greater diversity of religious groups than any other country in the world. From the usual suspects (Christianity, Judaism, Hinduism, Buddhism, and Islam) to the more off-beat (Theosophy, Hare Krishna, Indian Shamanism, Scientology, voodoo, Wicca, Edward Cayce's New Age nonsense, and those guys who dance with snakes), we've got all the bases covered, and it's all protected by the First Amendment.

On the other hand, if you don't believe any of it, you have the God-given right to be a complete atheist and *still* take Christmas off, dammit!

THANKSGIVING

We've got a lot to be thankful for . . . like food. Our country has a lot of it.

In 1621, after a four-month journey on the *Mayflower*, a really shitty winter, scurvy, and pneumonia, half of the original 102 pilgrims who'd landed at Plymouth were history. Nevertheless, thanks to a successful harvest and help from a guy named Squanto, they were ready to party. Ninety-one Native Americans were invited, and for three days everyone feasted on goose, duck, venison, lobsters, mashed cranberries, clams, bass, corn, veggies, and dried fruit. (Turkey and pumpkin pie were later additions.)

The trend didn't catch on until 1863, when Abe Lincoln proclaimed Thanksgiving a national holiday, creating a distinctly American tradition. Now, once a year, millions of Americans break their diets to stuff their faces to excess on turkey, mashed potatoes, and stuffing. They sit on the couch, digest, and resume stuffing.

Fortunately, we also invented Alka-Seltzer.

FUN FACTS

Nikki's Kids

Sergei Khrushchev, the son of a Soviet Cold War crusader, not only teaches at Brown University, but recently became a U.S. citizen. Said Sergei: "It's a great country and it's an honor to live here." Pretty funny, since his dad once pounded his shoe against a table at the United Nations and proclaimed to the world, "We will bury you!"

THE STATUE
OF LIBERTY

Since we haven't been around as long as everyone else, we've been playing catch-up in the monument department. Maybe that's why each and every one of ours makes a big, bold statement.

And the mother of all American monuments is undoubtedly the Statue of Liberty. She's tall, she's beautiful, and she's built like a hot French chick! She has also come to symbolize freedom to people everywhere around the world.

A gift from France in recognition of the friendship between our two nations, Lady Liberty was dedicated on Liberty Island, New York, on October 28, 1886. The statue itself was built by the French, but we built and paid for the pedestal. In order to help foot the bill, Jewish-American poet Emma Lazarus wrote and auctioned off her famous poem, which was later inscribed at the statue's base: "Give me your tired, your poor, Your huddled masses yearning to breathe free, The wretched refuse of your teeming shore. Send these, the homeless, tempest-tossed to me. I lift my lamp beside the golden door!"

Pretty deep, huh?! More than just a pretty face, this broad's got brains.

THE STATUE OF LIBERTY'S VITAL STATS:

SWF

HEIGHT: *151 feet, 1 inch*

WEIGHT: *almost 200 tons*

LIKES: *carrying a torch, open-toed sandals, nice views, hats, meeting new people*

FUN FACTS

Nothing Monumental About It . . .

As we all know from high school, Plymouth Rock is where the pilgrims landed, setting up the first American colony in Plymouth, Massachusetts. While this alone makes Plymouth a pretty big fucking deal as a historic site, first-time visitors might be disappointed to find that it pretty much lives up to its name. It's a rock—well, maybe a boulder—and that's about it. Frankly, the gift shop is bigger than the main attraction. Ahhh . . . capitalism at its best.

Other Big Monuments That Rule!

LINCOLN MEMORIAL

Located in the heart of our nation's capital, you really can't appreciate the majesty of Lincoln kickin' it in his chair until you see him in person. The memorial's cornerstone was laid in 1915 on Abe's birthday by architect Henry Bacon and sculptor Daniel French, and the finished product was finally dedicated in 1922 by Chief Justice William Howard Taft, whose weight at the time was comparable to that of the statues. The Lincoln Memorial has since been the staging ground for some of the most important rallies in U.S. history. Indeed, it was from this auspicious setting that Martin Luther King gave his famous "I Have a Dream" speech to commemorate the centennial of the Emancipation Proclamation. Abe would've been proud.

MOUNT RUSHMORE

Americans like things BIG, and you can't get much bigger than having your mug implanted on the side of a whole friggin' mountain! Standing in the Black Hills of western South Dakota, Mount Rushmore is a whopping 5,600 feet high, and features the likenesses of George Washington, Thomas Jefferson, Abraham Lincoln, and Theodore Roosevelt. It's been a dramatic setting for countless Hollywood blockbusters, including the chase scene in *North by Northwest*. Yes, someone has to clean Jefferson's nose from time to time. And yes, like so many real Americans, all the forefathers have had at least one facelift.

RANDY'S DONUTS

Flying into Los Angeles International Airport, if you peek out the window, you can't miss the giant donut sitting atop the roof of this local institution. The donut itself, modeled after a plain old-fashioned, no glaze, was designed by Robert Graham in 1953 for owner Russ Wendell, who envisioned a chain of over 100 donut-crowned shops. Well, that didn't quite work out. But we still have the original, located on La Cienega and Manchester. It's appeared in numerous films, television shows, and print ads alike. And the giant donut has friends all across the United States: Paul Bunyan, holding a tire or miniature golf putter in his grip, the world's largest artichoke, huge balls of twine, a colossal thermometer, and many other examples of the American belief that size, indeed, does matter.

Even More U.S. Monuments That Rule...

Albert Einstein (DC)

Big Green Monster (MA)

Biggest Disco Ball (CA)

Biggest Guitar (IN)

Biggest Rubber-Band Ball (DE)

Crazy Horse (SD)

de Soto Statue (FL)

Edgar Allan Poe (PA)

Edison (NJ)

Eisenhower (PA)

Eleanor Roosevelt (NY)

FDR Memorial (DC)

Fort Bowie (AZ)

Fort Scott (KS)

Frederick Douglass (DC)

Friendship Hill (PA)

George Washington Carver (MO)

Golden Spike (UT)

Grant's Tomb (NY)

Iwo Jima (VA)

Jimmy Carter (GA)

John Muir (CD)

John Paul Jones Memorial (DC)

Largest U.S. Flag (CA)

Longfellow Statue (MA)

Lyndon B. Johnson Memorial (TX)

Minuteman (MA)

Old North Church (MA)

St. Louis Arch (MO)

Thomas Jefferson Memorial (DC)

Tuskegee Airmen (AL)

Thomas Stone (MD)

Washington Monument (DC)

Whitman Mission (WA)

Wright Brothers (NC)

Vietnam Veterans Memorial (DC)

THE
OLD WEST

America without the Old West would be like England without all that knight and castle crap. Though the time period of the Old West and Expansionism was only about fifty years, its mythology lives on to this day, rife with tales of good guys against bad guys, stagecoaches, claim-jumpers, posses, saloons, and gunfights.

How do we know so much about this thin sliver of American history? Hollywood, of course! Just as *M*A*S*H* lasted longer than the Korean War, thousands upon thousands of Westerns—starring fake cowboys like John Wayne, Roy Rogers, Henry Fonda, and Clint Eastwood—have kept names like Wyatt, Butch, and Sundance alive for over a century.

Our love for the Old West, and our desire to preserve it on film, is simple: The open range symbolizes freedom and opportunity, from that undeveloped plot of land to build a homestead on, to that struggling ranch overrun by rustlers, to the vein of gold in them there hills.

Oh, and just for the record, Custer had it coming to him.

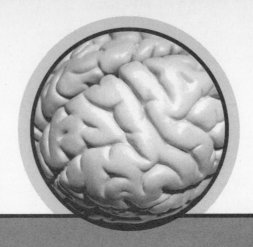

REASON
14

BRAINS

Okay, maybe not all of us are smart (have you ever been to a NASCAR event?), but we have had more than our share of brainiacs. Even those geniuses who immigrated here came up with some of their best theories on U.S. soil.

We may not have as many philosophers as the Greeks, British, or Germans, but our great thinkers don't just sit on their duffs and talk shit. Our top-shelf intellectuals are doers, not afraid to get in the trenches, soil their hands, and come up with ways to turn their theories into practical applications. $E = MC^2$. Electricity. The Krispy Kreme Old-Fashioned Glazed. All products of American ingenuity.

> "A mind is a terrible thing to waste."
> —United Negro College Fund slogan
>
> "What a waste it is to lose one's mind.
> Or not to have a mind is being very wasteful.
> How true that is."
> —Vice President Dan Quayle to the NAACP

Great American Minds

ALBERT EINSTEIN

Have you ever heard the phrase "You're no Einstein"? Well, he was. Once you've become the euphemism for being smart, you've got it made! German-born, Einstein emigrated to the United States when Adolf Hitler was elected Chancellor of Germany. They didn't want him, but America did. He won a Nobel prize for his explanation of the photoelectric effect, AKA the theory of relativity ($E = MC^2$). Considered by many to be one of the fathers of the atomic bomb, Einstein in his later life was active in the cause of international disarmament. Ironically, despite all his brain power, he still couldn't figure out how to comb his hair!

BENJAMIN FRANKLIN

It's all about the Benjamin, baby! Known to most as the guy on the C-note, Franklin was a classic Renaissance man, making huge accomplishments as an inventor (the lightning rod, bifocal glasses, daylight savings), writer/publisher (*Poor Richard's Almanac*), statesman (he helped craft the Constitution), founder (the Library of Congress, the Post Office), and he still found the time to bang lots of chicks. One of his mistresses was heard to say, "He wasn't called 'lightning rod Ben' because he invented it." Indeed, he was the Bill Clinton of his day, and it is said that the eyes of his statue in Philadelphia leer at passing women. He is considered one of this nation's greatest Founding Playboys, er, Fathers.

BEN STEIN

Originally a speechwriter for Richard Nixon, Ben Stein maintains that he did not write the "I am not a crook" line. A genius at marketing his own nerdiness, Ben is a trained lawyer and professor, and has written over fifteen books, including *A License to Steal: Michael Milken and the Conspiracy to Bilk the Nation* and *The View from Sunset Boulevard*. Late-night TV fans might also have heard of a great old show called *Fernwood 2-Night* that BS helped create. Non-late-night fans know Ben as the short, smart guy with glasses and a funny voice on the aptly named *Win Ben Stein's Money*. We still love his movie-stealing role in *Ferris Beuller's Day Off.* "Beuller? Beuller?"

American Nobel Prize Winners

The United States has won more Nobel Prizes (249) than any other nation. It breaks down like this: Physics (69), Chemistry (45), Medicine (80), Literature (10), Peace (18), and Economics (27). Here are some recent U.S. winners:

Saul Bellow (Lit)

Walter H. Brattain (Phys)

Steven Chu (Phys)

Robert F. Furchgott (Med)

Paul Greengard (Med)

James Heckman (Econ)

Alan J. Heeger (Chem)

Eric Kandel (Med)

Jack S. Kilby (Phys)

Herbert Kroemer (Phys)

Robert B. Laughlin (Phys)

Robert E. Lucas (Econ)

George Marshall (Peace)

Daniel L. McFadden (Econ)

Robert C. Merton (Econ)

Toni Morrison (Lit)

John F. Nash (Econ)

Carl Linus Pauling (Phys)

William D. Phillips (Phys)

Myron S. Scholes (Econ)

William Shockly (Phys)

Richard E. Smalley (Chem)

John Steinbeck (Lit)

Daniel C. Tsui (Phys)

Jody Williams (Peace)

THE POST OFFICE

Neither snow nor rain nor heat nor gloom of night stays these couriers from the swift completion of their appointed rounds," goes the saying. It's true. Thanks to the U.S. Postal Service, your letter can journey from Key West, Florida, to Nome, Alaska, all for the price of a stamp.

When Congress named Ben Franklin the first Postmaster General in 1775, we were a ragtag confederation of scattered colonies. The postal system bound the new nation together, aided the growth of commerce, and promoted a free flow of ideas. In two-hundred-plus years, it's grown into a first-class operation studied and mimicked across the globe. Each year, 800,000 postal workers deliver more than 200 billion pieces of mail to 250 million Americans at 134 million addresses. We carry more mail to more people over a larger geographic area than any other country in the world.

Ever live abroad? It can take over a month just to get a letter. But here in the U.S.A., you can count on the mailman coming six days a week like clockwork, delivering everything from postcards to paychecks to that highly anticipated copy of *Playboy*.

THE DOLLAR

There's a reason they call it the "almighty dollar."

It might not be the prettiest or the most colorful, but our moola is the worldwide standard. It's not based on gold or silver, but rather the basic stability of our nation's economy. U.S. greenbacks are simply the safest currency in the world, accepted virtually everywhere!

Know anybody who invests heavily in the peso or Euro? Neither do we. Even our enemies find comfort in keeping their savings in American banks—hey, would you trust your hard-earned dough in the local Iraqi bank? Didn't think so. Moreover, who in their right mind would want to go to an Iraqi ATM in the middle of the night?

DEAD PRESIDENTS...

There are over 4,000,000,000 $1 bills
in circulation, and the life expectancy of each
buck is only about eighteen months.

MAJOR ERECTIONS

From Lincoln Logs to the Lincoln Tunnel, Americans like erecting stuff. Cool stuff. Big stuff. Lots of stuff. Hell, we built a kickass nation in just over two centuries! We built the world's longest transcontinental railroad track by track, spike by spike. We moved 260,000,000 cubic yards of earth amidst malaria and heat and yellow fever to build the Panama Canal.

We've constructed some of the world's most impressive buildings. New York and Chicago each have more skyscrapers than any city in any country. And we built the largest mall in the world. Meanwhile, architects like Frank Gehry, Frank Lloyd Wright, and Chinese-American I. M. Pei are known across the globe for their innovative designs.

We've created giant mirrored pyramids, offices that look like stacks of LPs, and restaurants shaped like giant brown derbies. We've made oases out of deserts, and have erected magnificent structures out of discarded bottles and cans and other refuse.

Not only that, Iowa's own Bryan Berg holds the world record for tallest house of cards—24 feet 10 inches, using 2,800 decks, and supporting four tons of weight. This dude clearly had way too much time on his hands.

Great Things Built in America!

GOLDEN GATE BRIDGE

What's the biggest erection in San Francisco? The Golden Gate Bridge. It's not the longest bridge in world, or even in the U.S. (the Verrazano Narrows in New York has it beat), but its majestic beauty is certainly world-renowned. Painted orange vermilion rather than gold, the 4,200-foot-long suspension bridge spans the Golden Gate Strait, the body of water connecting the San Francisco Bay to the Pacific Ocean. Chief engineer Joseph B. Strauss started construction in 1933, and completed it in '37. As of 2000, 1,634,141,491 vehicles had crossed the bridge. This includes the vehicle of Jefferson Airplane's Grace Slick, who crashed into one of the bridge's retaining walls during a drunken drag race in '71. She wasn't killed, but others haven't been so lucky. In the past 64 years, over 1,000 people have jumped off the Golden Gate, making it the most popular suicide destination on the planet.

THE EMPIRE STATE BUILDING

It's no longer the biggest building out there, but it remains a symbol of America's race to the top. After the French built the Eiffel Tower in 1889, the competition was on to build the world's next tallest building. New York was up for the fight. First up was the Metropolitan Life Tower in 1909, followed by the Woolworth Building in 1913, and the Bank of Manhattan Building in 1929. None were larger than the Eiffel. But when automobile moguls Walter Chrysler and John Raskob (General Motors) got into the erectile cockfight in 1931, things got ugly. When Chrysler added some stories, so too did Raskob. In the end, Raskob's was bigger. Built in one year and forty-five days at a cost of over $40 million, his Empire State Building had 102 stories and stood 1,224 feet tall (1,454 if you count the lightning rod). It not only became the world's tallest building at the time, but also the architectural ambassador for our country. King Kong liked it so much that he climbed it in 1933. He took the short way down.

Even More Erections That Rule...

Allegheny Tunnel, PA

Anton Anderson Memorial Tunnel, AK

Baltimore Harbor Tunnel, MD

Baton Rouge Bridge, LA

Bradbury Building, CA

Bronx-Whitestone Bridge, NY

Brooklyn Battery Tunnel, NY

Capitol Records Building, CA

Cathedral of St. John the Divine, NY

Chrysler Building, NY

Delaware Memorial Bridge, DE

Eisenhower Tunnel, CO

Fort McHenry Tunnel, MD

Fort Peck Dam, MT

Fort Randall Dam, SD

George Washington Bridge, NY

Gramercy Bridge, LA

Greater New Orleans Bridges, LA

Hampton Roads Tunnel, VA

Holland Tunnel, NY/NJ

Hoover Dam, NV

LBJ Tunnel, TX

Lincoln Tunnel, NY

Mackinac Straits Bridge, MI

Mission Tailings, AZ

New Cornelia Tailings Dam, AZ

Oahe Dam, SD

Oroville Dam, CA

Even More Erections That Rule...

Queens-Midtown Tunnel, NY

Rockefeller Center, NY

San Francisco–Oakland Bay Bridge, CA

San Luis Dam, CA

Sears Tower, Chicago

Seaway Skyway Bridge, NY

Sideling Hill Tunnel, PA

Singer Building, NY

Space Needle, WA

Tacoma Narrows II Bridge, WA

Thimble Shoal Tunnel, PA

Ted Williams Tunnel, MA

Trump Tower, NY

Verrazano-Narrows Bridge, NY

Walt Whitman Bridge, PA

Woolworth Building, NY

Great Things Built in America!

THE MALL OF AMERICA

What do you do when both your professional football and baseball teams move downtown? If you live in Minnesota, you turn their old stadiums into the largest shopping and retail center the world has ever seen. So was born the Mall of America. And let us tell you, the place is freakin' huge! In 1992, it opened its doors with 2.5 million square feet of retail space. It now features over 520 retail stores, employs 12,000 people, and gets 35 to 42 million visitors a year. Along with all the retail stores, the MOA has its very own roller coaster, a giant aquarium with more than 3,000 sea critters, a bowling alley (duh, it's in Minnesota), movie theaters, and a nightclub. While the parking lot is generous, God help you if you forget where you parked.

FUN FACTS

We Got the Biggest!

America's Baywatch *is the biggest syndicated TV show in the world, racking up 1.1 billion viewers weekly in 162 countries.*

THE GREAT AMERICAN NOVEL

The Great American Novel is to the aspiring writer what the American Dream is to the average American.

We're a young country, and while we have folks like Jack London, William Faulkner, and Ernest Hemingway (who've all written Great American Novels), we don't have the same literary history as places like England or France. That means that an unknown scribe actually has a shot at grabbing a place in the lexicon of American literature, and having his or her words pored over for generations. Each year, American writers pen thousands of books in pursuit of this Holy Grail of fiction.

In addition, America is directly responsible for free verse poetry (Walt Whitman), hard-boiled detective fiction (Dashiell Hammett), modern science fiction (Isaac Asimov), and gonzo journalism (Hunter S. Thompson). Our writers are risk-takers and heartbreakers.

We also invented Cliffs Notes.

Even More American Scribes Who Rule...

Forrest James Ackerman

Louisa May Alcott

Isaac Asimov

Jean Auel

Saul Bellow

David Barry

Alfred Bester

Ambrose Bierce

Harold Bloom

Judy Blume

David Borgenicht

Anthony Bourdain

Paul Bowles

T. C. Boyle

Ray Bradbury

Lilian Jackson Braun

Richard Brautigan

Charles Bukowski

Edgar Rice Burroughs

William S. Burroughs

James M. Cain

Truman Capote

Caleb Carr

Raymond Carver

Willa Cather

Raymond Chandler

John Cheever

Sandra Cisneros

American Writers Who Rule!

MARK TWAIN

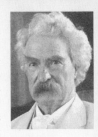

Born Samuel Clemens, Mark Twain was one of the first American smartass writers and humorists, chain-smoking cigars and making fun of people whenever he felt like it. Where would America be without Twain defining what being a kid was all about? His books include *The Adventures of Tom Sawyer, The Prince and the Pauper, A Connecticut Yankee in King Arthur's Court,* and *The Adventures of Huck Finn.* While every high school English teacher makes you read his books, they'd probably never want you to hang out with the man—lest you develop some bad habits.

ERNEST HEMINGWAY

Without this fine semi-expatriate writer icon, America would still be looking for its paradigmatic larger-than-life, hard-living, hard-drinking man's man. God bless him! Emily Dickinson's evil opposite, Hemingway wrote with a simplicity of language that laid to waste all the Victorian fluff of the era. Anyone could read and enjoy a Hemingway book without a dictionary. He won the Pulitzer Prize in 1953 for *The Old Man and the Sea* and the Nobel the next year. Though he died in 1961 of the classic "self-inflicted gunshot wound," his legacy lives on with consistent sales of his books and the yearly "Best of Bad Hemingway" competition.

STEPHEN KING

Never has one man scared the crap out of so many. King has written scores of books, had a bunch of them turned into movies, and still manages to sneak in a few touching novels here and there. While we love his words, we do feel badly for his kids, who probably didn't look forward to Daddy reading them a bedtime story every sleepless night. Our favorite King classics include *Carrie, The Shining, The Stand, The Dead Zone, Cujo,* and *Christine.* While the writing's great, the movie adaptations are sometimes a bit sketchy. Did we really need to see an eye-patched George C. Scott in *Firestarter?* You can also catch King playing guitar in his band, The Rock Bottom Remainders.

American Writers Who Rule!

JACK LONDON

Adventure books wouldn't be the same without good ol' Jack telling bright-eyed lads about life on the sea and the frozen tundra. London was born in San Francisco in 1876, spent time as an oyster pirate on a schooner, and traveled around the United States as a hobo. A self-educated man, he was said to read and write up to twenty hours a day. When he was twenty-one, he hit the Klondike during the gold rush; two years later he started to publish short stories and then books. London lived it, then wrote about it. His most famous works include *The Call of the Wild* and *White Fang.*

WALT WHITMAN

If you read the works of one great American poet, this should probably be the guy, though nobody *really* reads poetry. The granddaddy of American verse, Whitman's opus *Leaves of Grass* stands at the forefront of great American writing. Without Whitman there would be no T. S. Eliot or Allen Ginsberg. Here's something you might not know: Whitman's "job" at the New York Attorney General's office—a job where he was expected NOT to do a stitch of official work—was given to him as a way to support his writing by his fan Teddy Roosevelt. Whitman was subsequently fired after *Leaves of Grass* was deemed an immoral work.

EMILY DICKINSON

She sure wrote some pretty stuff for a chick who never left the house. Dickinson was born, lived, and died in Amherst, Massachusetts, from 1830 to 1886. She published very little during her lifetime, and what she did put out was done anonymously, so she never cashed in on the residuals from her millions of books sold. While poets like Whitman threw away tradition and wrote of the open road, Dickinson stuck with traditional poetic structure and wrote about the closed doors, penning some 1,775 poems and a ton of letters. You probaby read her most famous poem, "Because I Could Not Stop for Death," in high school.

Even More American Scribes Who Rule...

Tom Clancy

Tom Clark

Beverly Cleary

Rob Cohen

Wanda Coleman

Gregory Corso

Stephen Crane

Robert Creeley

Michael Crichton

e. e. cummings

Don DeLillo

Nelson DeMille

Philip K. Dick

Franklin W. Dixon

Diane DiPrima

E. L. Doctorow

Ignatius Donnelly

Theodore Dreiser

T. S. Eliot

Ralph Waldo Emerson

Lawrence Ferlinghetti

F. Scott Fitzgerald

Barton Fink

Jonathan Franzen

Betty Friedan

John Gardner

David Goodes

Even More American Scribes Who Rule...

Edward Gorey

Zane Grey

John Grisham

Alex Haley

Thomas Harris

Jim Harrison

Nathaniel Hawthorne

Robert Heinlein

Joseph Heller

Lillian Hellman

O. Henry

Frank Herbert

Langston Hughes

Carl Hiaasen

David Ignatow

Henry James

Robinson Jeffers

LeRoi Jones

Bob Kaufman

Jack Kerouac

Ken Kesey

Barbara Kingsolver

Maxine Hong Kingston

Dean Koontz

Gary Larson

Louis L'Amour

H. P. Lovecraft

Rick Lupert

American Writers Who Rule!

DASHIELL HAMMETT

A detective for the Pinkerton company, Hammett utilized the lessons he learned along with his great talent for succinct rough-and-tough narrative to put his mark on American literary history. One of the inventors of the hard-boiled detective genre, along with Raymond Chandler, Hammett created private detective Sam Spade in *The Maltese Falcon*, as well as the Manhattan drinking society detectives Nora and Nick Charles in *The Thin Man*. If you head to his hometown of San Francisco, you can go to one of his favorite watering holes, John's Grill in Union Square, and enjoy a few of the great martinis that fueled his alcohol-induced writing style, and ultimately led to his early death.

WILLIAM FAULKNER

Love or hate his dense, long-winded, stream-of-consciousness prose, you gotta admit, the dude could write. A raging alcoholic who managed to drop out of both high school and college, he nevertheless scored a Nobel Prize for literature. Career highlights including *The Sound and the Fury, As I Lay Dying, Absolom, Absolom,* and *Go Down Moses* helped him win it. On the other hand, his screenplay adaptations of "lesser" writers, including Hemingway's *To Have And Have Not* and Chandler's *The Big Sleep,* actually made him some bank, but he hated doing it. A fictionalized Faulkner popped up in the Coen brothers movie *Barton Fink*.

ALLEN GINSBERG

Like most famous writers, he dropped out of college. Okay, so he was kicked out. Who cares?! While Jack Kerouac stole most of the glory during the height of the Beat Generation days with books like *On the Road* and *The Subterraneans,* Allen Ginsburg is really the era's premier scribe. Though inspired by the works of Ezra Pound and Walt Whitman, he was also influenced by jazz, his words jumping from the page like never before. Choice works include *Howl* (about the Beats), *Kaddish* (about his crazy dead mom), and *Reality Sandwich* (you'll have to read

American Writers Who Rule!

that yourself). Ginsberg was also an avid antiwar activist, Buddhist, and vegetarian, and recorded a cool song with The Clash.

DR. SEUSS

Who woulda thought that a kid who flunked art
would twang such a chord in our country's dear heart?
Born Theodor Geisel in Springfield, Mass.,
he started at *Time* magazine, but alas, political satire made him quite melancholic
(his drawings were just too goddamn hyperbolic).
So he thought up a plan, and he thought it up quick,
"With the prefix of doctor, I'll sound mighty slick."
And so it was that Dr. Seuss
became the tightest rhyme-slinger since Mother Goose.
The Grinch, Sneetch, and Lorax? All allegory,
talking smack about materialism, racism, and ecology.
Then there was that persnickity Cat—
you know, the iconoclastic rule-breaker in the tall Hat?
He was a far cry from Dick and that vapid bitch Jane,
but made learning to read a lot less mundane.

ALICE WALKER

Along with writers like Zora Neale Hurston, Toni Morrison, and Wanda Coleman, Alice Walker helped to chronicle the female condition in black America. Born in Eatonton, Georgia, in 1944, Walker was active in the Civil Rights movement in the 1960s. Though her previous books had been well received, it wasn't until she published *The Color Purple* in 1982 that Walker's works were firmly established on most required reading lists. *The Color Purple* won both the American Book Award and the Pulitzer Prize for fiction but more important, it stayed on the *New York Times* bestseller list for twenty-five weeks and was made into a major motion picture by Steven Spielberg. Alice Walker continues to write great books including *The Temple of My Familiar* and the children's book *Langston Hughes: American Poet.*

Even More American Scribes Who Rule...

Ross Macdonald

Norman Mailer

David Mamet

Robin Masters

Peter Matthiessen

Herman Melville

H. L. Mencken

Arthur Miller

Henry Miller

Vladimir Nabokov

Joyce Carol Oates

Ogden Nash

Flannery O'Connor

Eugene O'Neill

Dorothy Parker

James Patterson

Joshua Piven

Sylvia Plath

Edgar Allan Poe

Katherine Anne Porter

Chaim Potok

Ezra Pound

Mario Puzo

Thomas Pynchon

Ishmael Reed

Anne Rice

Tom Robbins

Even More American Scribes Who Rule...

Philip Roth

J. D. Salinger

Carl Sandburg

William Saroyan

Delmore Schwartz

Charles M. Schulz

J. Otto Seibold

Maurice Sendak

Anne Sexton

Ntozake Shange

Sidney Sheldon

Sam Shepard

Shel Silverstein

Isaac Bashevis Singer

Snoopy

Danielle Steel

Gertrude Stein

John Steinbeck

Jim Thompson

Henry David Thoreau

James Thurber

Kilgore Trout

Scott Turow

John Updike

Gore Vidal

American Writers Who Rule!

DAVID SEDARIS

This space was originally slated for Herman Melville, but although many consider *Moby Dick* to be the greatest American novel ever, we fucking hated reading it in high school. On the other hand, David Sedaris's strange-but-true, utterly irreverent, autobiographical short stories are always a hoot. Audiences got their first taste of Sedaris when he read about his experiences as a Macy's elf on National Public Radio. Big on sarcasm, self-effacing humor, and cutting social commentary, Sedaris has been compared to Mark Twain, Dorothy Parker, and even Woody Allen, and has penned the bestsellers *Barrel Fever, Naked, Holiday on Ice*, and *Me Talk Pretty Someday*. No, he never worked on a whaling boat, but we hear Dave knows a thing or two about moby dicks.

Judith Viorst

Kurk Vonnegut

Dian Wakoski

Alice Walker

Vivian Walsh

Pam Ward

Booker T. Washington

Nathanael West

Edith Wharton

Walt Whitman

E. B. White

Elie Wiesel

Tennessee Williams

William Carlos Williams

Tom Wolfe

David Wollock

Richard Wright

TOILET PAPER

In 1857, New Yorker Joseph Gayetti created the first packaged toilet paper. The Scott brothers picked up where he left off, and our asses have never been the same since.

Talk to any Russian and ask them for a list of things they covet from the West. Right next to grain, they might just add good ol' American TP—arguably the most squeezable on the planet.

It's soft, it's quilted, and it comes in assorted styles and colors. Take a trip to any Third World country, eat a plate of curry, wash it down with some local H_2O, and you'll most certainly miss one of the things that make our country great. Our shit stinks as much as everyone else's, but our butts sure as hell are less "chafed."

THE INSIDE POOP ...

Before TP, people cleaned their business with newspaper, hayballs, sheep's wool, grass, corncobs, the Sears catalog, your left hand and some water, and other uncomfy fare.

CORN FLAKES

Most of us grew up on cold cereal, whether it was Special K or Count Chocula. Just open box, pour in bowl, add milk. And most of us are familiar with the childhood ritual of fishing through the box for the prize. But cold cereal wasn't always "part of a complete breakfast." Back in the day, breakfast was all about hot porridge or gruel. Bleechh!

In the 1800s, a New York doctor named James Jackson came up with the idea of cold cereal—a granular bran he called Granula—designed to keep folks fit and regular. But it was health nut Dr. John Kellogg, owner/operator of a Battle Creek, Michigan, health resort, who put cold cereal on the map with his Battle Creek Health Foods in the 1890s. The first product he offered was Granola, followed, in 1907, by the now-ubiquitous Corn Flakes.

Today, Kellogg's is a staple in millions of American pantries nationwide. Boasting annual sales of $9 billion and marketed in over 160 countries, it's the world's leading producer of cereal.

FUN FACTS

10 Great Ways to Start Your Day!

Forget Mueslix and gruel; try some of our favorite American breakfast cereals!

- ★ Boo Berry
- ★ Cap'n Crunch with Crunchberries
- ★ Cinnamon Life
- ★ Cocoa Puffs
- ★ Cookie Crisp
- ★ Count Chocula
- ★ Frosted Flakes
- ★ Lucky Charms
- ★ Trix
- ★ Wheaties

THE GRAND CANYON

We may be the third most populated country in the world, but we have three times as many national parks as anyone else, and the largest amount of protected wildlife area (900,000 square miles) of anyone. And when it comes to American natural wonders, none is more iconic than the Grand Canyon.

Carved out by the Colorado River, covering 1,218,375 acres, and plunging 6,000 feet at its deepest point, it's essentially a big-ass hole in the ground. But oh, what a hole! The strata of ancient red, brown and black rocks in the canyon's walls, which change with the light throughout the day, are a sight to behold. Native American pictographs whisk you back in time. And seventy-five species of mammals, fifty species of reptiles and amphibians, twenty-five species of fish, and 300 species of birds, including the endangered bald eagle, all call the Grand Canyon home.

With five million visitors every year, it's the classic American vacay destination. Heck, even the Bradys and Griswolds marveled at its beauty!

National Parks That Rule...

ACADIA

BADLANDS

BIG BEND

BIG CYPRESS

BIG THICKET

BLACK CANYON ON THE GUNNISON

BRYCE CANYON

CAPITOL REEFS

CARLSBAD CAVERNS

CRATER LAKE

CUYAHOGA VALLEY

DEATH VALLEY

DRY TORTUGAS

EVERGLADES

GATES OF THE ARCTIC

GLACIER

GLACIER BAY

GREAT SAND DUNES

GREAT SMOKY MOUNTAINS

GUADALUPE MOUNTAINS

HALEAKALA

JOSHUA TREE

LAKE CLARK

LITTLE RIVER CANYON

MAMMOTH CAVE

MESA VERDE

MOJAVE

NOATAK HOT SPRINGS PETRIFIED FOREST

PRINCE WILLIAM FOREST

REDWOOD

ROCKY MOUNTAIN

SAGUARO

SEQUOIA

SHENANDOAH

THEODORE ROOSEVELT

WRANGELL-ST. ELIAS

ZION

More Natural Treasures

YOSEMITE NATIONAL PARK

Each year, big rocks, big trees, and big waterfalls beckon over four million visitors to Yosemite, located in California's central Sierra Nevada. In 1864, President Lincoln declared Yosemite Valley and the Mariposa Grove of Giant Sequoias an inalienable public trust. Later, long-haired bearded mountain man John Muir fought to save the meadows surrounding the valley, resulting in the creation of Yosemite National Park in 1890. Today, the park is home to over 2,000 varieties of plants and wildlife, as well as an abundant variety of camera-toting Japanese tourists.

YELLOWSTONE NATIONAL PARK

Established in 1872, Yellowstone National Park is the first and oldest national park in the world, encompassing over 3,400 square miles in three states. Since it opened, over 120 million tourists have stopped by to look at Yellowstone's 10,000 hot springs and geysers (such as Old Faithful), and the largest concentration of free-roaming wildlife in the lower forty-eight states. The place is like a zoo without bars—you can't spit without hitting some sort of animal, whether it's a moose, beaver, bison, whooping crane, bald eagle, mountain lion, grizzly bear, or any number of other critters that might break into your car or eat small children.

JELLYSTONE NATIONAL PARK

Discovered in 1958, Jellystone became a popular destination throughout the '60s. Visitors came in droves to enjoy the park's spouting geysers and unique species of talking wildlife. In fact, the park's profile was greatly increased by the high jinks of one particular bear, often spotted in his natural habitat sporting a blue cap and necktie. When a rash of stolen picnic baskets threatened tourism, hard-nosed ranger John Smith was called in to handle what he described as "smarter than the average bear... always getting in my hair." In one spectacular act of bravado, the bear was said to have commandeered a helicopter to swoop down on unsuspecting picnickers.

FUN FACTS

People magazine . . .

. . . is our country's biggest weekly news magazine. If the total number of issues of *People* sold to date—somewhere just under 4 billion—were laid end to end at the equator, they would circle the earth 26.6 times.

AFRICAN
AMERICANS

Face it: If you're black, you know you're cool, and if you're not black, at one time or another you wished you were.

African Americans have virtually defined "hip" in our country, creating blues, jazz, rock 'n' roll and hip-hop—and all the slanguage, dances, and clothing styles that have come along with them. A huge percentage of our greatest athletes, from Jesse Owens to Tiger Woods, are also black.

Black contributions are not limited to entertainment and sports, either. Langston Hughes, Richard Wright, W. E. B. Du Bois, and Ishmael Reed greatly impacted our literary tradition. Spike Lee is one of the most innovative filmmakers of his time. And Sam Jackson is just about the baddest muthafucka on the planet.

The traffic light, peanut products, and filament in lightbulbs were all invented by African Americans. An entire cuisine can be attributed to African Americans, from grits to gumbo. The Roebuck of Sears & Roebuck was black. And Rosa Parks, the Tuskeegee Airman, Frederick Douglass, Harriet Tubman, and Malcolm X all shaped our history as much as any of our nation's heroes.

Solid.

SUSAN B. ANTHONY

Her friends never called her Giggles, she was never the life of the party, and she didn't date much. See, little Susie had a bone to pick. She knew that all men *and* women were created equal...even if the Founding Fathers forgot to mention it.

Born on February 15, 1820, Anthony was brought up in a politically active Quaker family. Though she fought hard as a member of the American Anti-Slavery Society, she was ticked when the slaves were freed, yet women remained unable to vote.

Along with Elizabeth Cady Stanton, Anthony founded the newspaper *The Revolution* in 1868, which advocated such newfangled ideas as the eight-hour workday, equal pay for equal work, and the advantages of buying American. In 1877, she brought Congress a petition for women's voting rights from twenty-six states with over 10,000 signatures—and was laughed at. But that still didn't stop her. She spoke before every Congress from 1869 to 1906 about women's suffrage. Anthony died in 1906 at her home in Rochester.

Like Moses, she never saw the Promised Land—the 19th Amendment giving women the right to vote—which was finally passed in 1920. On the other hand, she *did* get her mug emblazoned on those shiny but useless silver dollars. It's the thought that counts....

American Women Who Rule!

ELEANOR ROOSEVELT

While her hubby, Franklin, was known for saying, "The only thing we have to fear is fear itself," Eleanor once expounded, "You gain strength, courage and confidence by every experience in which you stop to look fear in the face." As First Lady, she set new precedents for women in politics: She was an outspoken advocate for the people suffering during the Great Depression, and many of her ideas were incorporated into FDR's New Deal programs. When FDR died, Mrs. Roosevelt's career in politics and social reform was just starting. Her greatest accomplishments were to help found UNICEF (the United Nations International Children's Emergency Fund) and to establish the Universal Declaration of Human Rights.

RUTH BADER GINSBURG

Judge Judy she's not. This chick is the real deal, appointed to the Supreme Court in 1993. Born in Brooklyn in 1933, Ginsburg attended Columbia and Harvard law schools, serving on the law review for both. She has taught law at Rutgers, the University of Amsterdam, Harvard Law School, and many other fine institutions. In 1971, R. B. G. was instrumental in starting the Women's Rights Project for the ACLU and litigated several major women's rights cases. Before being appointed to the Supreme Court, she was a judge on the U.S. Court of Appeals. Here's a bit of irony: Ginsberg applied to be a clerk for Supreme Court Justice Felix Frankfurter but was not interviewed for the job because she was a woman. What a weenie!

More American Girl Power...

Madeleine Albright

Jane Amsterdam

Linda Bloodworth-Thomason

Clara Bow

Pearl S. Buck

Cagney & Lacey

Connie Chung

Barbara Cohen-Wolfe

Joan Didion

Emma Goldman

Sherry Lansing

Dolly Madison

Carol Mosley-Braun

Constance Baker Motley

Lucretia Mott

Jackie O

Annie Oakley

Sandra Day O'Connor

Dorothy Parker

Mary Pickford

Rosa Parks

Pocahontas

Bonnie Raitt

Cokie Roberts

More American Girl Power...

Margaret Roth

Dr. Ruth

Deborah Sills

Jamie Sommers

Gertrude Stein

Gloria Steinem

Harriet Tubman

Oprah Winfrey

Christine Todd Whitman

Esther Wollock-Wolf

Wonder Woman

BUFFY THE VAMPIRE SLAYER

This sexy blonde mall rat from Sunny-vale, CA, takes no crap. In 1997, at a mere 15 years old, she discovered that her sleepy town was built atop the por-tal to Hell, and soon switched her focus from ice skating and cheerleading to saving the world from vampires, demons, and other unsavory creatures. In the past five years, she's had a lot of shitty luck: Buffy's parents got divorced, she lost Mom to a brain tumor, she's had countless dates from hell (literally), and she was killed and brought back to life. Despite these trials and tribulations, she still shows up faithfully every week to entertain millions of fans nationwide. Her dedication, super-human strength, and adroit fighting skills are testa-ments to American Girl power. Plus, she's hot.

LEVI'S

You can take your ascot, your lame trousers, and your formal wear with constricting vests, and give us a pair of well-worn jeans any day.

Bavarian-born Levi Strauss came to San Francisco during the California Gold Rush to sell canvas for tents. Instead, he discovered that what the miners really needed was a good pair of pants that didn't rip apart on the job. Thus were born Levi's jeans.

Levi eventually switched from canvas to denim and dyed the pants blue to make sure they had a nice even color. Sold virtually everywhere, Levi jeans are coveted for their looks, comfort, and durability. More importantly, they look great on a nice, tight tushy.

VITAL STATS

Levi Strauss is the world's biggest brand-name clothing maker. Levi's are sold in more than 30,000 stores in sixty countries, with sales in excess of $6 billion. Now, that's a lotta pants!

THE ELECTRIC WASHING MACHINE

Doing laundry sucks ass, but imagine how much more it would suck ass if you had to scrub your clothes against a rock or piece of metal, by hand.

The first American to patent a washing machine using a drum was James King in 1851. In 1858, Hamilton Smith upped the washing ante with the rotary washing machine. William Blackstone had an even better idea. As a gift for his wife, he built her the first washing machine for use in the home.

While all of these machines were cool, you still had to crank the clothes through a series of wringers. Electricity changed that. In 1908, the Hurley Machine Company of Chicago introduced the first electric-powered washing machine. Finally, in 1947, the first top-loading automatic washer was invented by the 1900 Corporation, which later morphed into Whirlpool.

If you're a fan of clean pants, shirts, and undies, you have to give it up for the American inventors who came up with the washing machine, though we still can't seem to figure out where that missing sock went.

FUN FACTS

Dirty Laundry

The first Laundromat was opened by a gold miner and a carpenter in California in 1851. Their 12-shirt machine was powered by ten donkeys. Those asses cleaned a lot of shit.

YOU CAN RUN AT THE SPEED OF LIGHT.

REASON
26

FORTUNE COOKIES

Confucius say, "Man who believe that fortune cookie come from China is foolish man indeed."

That's right, folks. The crunchy folded cookies you munch after your egg rolls, won ton soup, kung pao chicken, and rice are as American as Thai Chicken Pizza.

As luck would have it, there are two conflicting stories as to the origins of this popular "Chinese" treat. In one, David Jung invented fortune cookies in L.A. in 1918 for unemployed men in need of a little pick-me-up. In another, the credit goes to Makoto Hagiwara, who supposedly started serving the cookies at San Francisco's Japanese Tea Garden in 1914. Fact of the matter is, fortune cookies were created on U.S. soil.

Furthermore, while Confucius may have penned some of the pithy, fortuitous sayings found on those little white slips of paper, he certainly didn't come up with the American convention of adding "... in bed" after each ancient pearl of wisdom.

"American" Foods That Rule

VICHYSSOISE (VISH-EE-SWAH)

Invented by a chef at New York's famed Ritz-Carlton hotel in 1917, Vichyssoise is essentially potato-leek soup with a fancy name. Here's the recipe: In a kettle, cook leeks and onions in butter over low heat, stirring occasionally, until they're mushy. Add potatoes, water, and salt. Simmer, covered, for 30 to 40 minutes, or until the potatoes are also soft. Add milk and bring the mixture just to a boil while stirring. In a food processor or blender, purée the mixture in batches, then strain through a very fine sieve into a bowl. Stir in cream and white pepper (for color) and chill. Garnish with chives and serve cold. Then tell your friends it's French so they'll think you're special.

CHOP SUEY

Chop suey was the food that symbolized "Chinese food" to a generation of Americans who didn't know any better. While the specific origins of chop suey are still debated, it's generally accepted that it was created by male Chinese immigrants who didn't know how to cook real Chinese food, either (their wives did the cooking), so they fudged a recipe, utilizing veggies and whatever meat was around. The name *chop suey* may have come from the Cantonese words meaning "mixed pieces." You can also add egg foo yung and subgum to the list of Chinese-American cuisine developed by 19th-century immigrants.

HÄAGEN-DAZS

This delicious treat was invented by a Jewish guy in the Bronx named Reuben Mattus. He sold his family's ice cream from age seventeen, but it wasn't until age forty-six that Mattus had a brainstorm: add more butterfat, use less air filler, and give the brand a fun, foreign-sounding name. He even stuck a map of Scandinavia on his original cartons, though the name has no meaning whatsoever in any language. Thus was born a new food category: superpremium ice cream. Mattus sold Häagen-Dazs to Pillsbury in 1993 for a ton of money, then, ironically, went on to work on a new low-fat ice cream. Simply dubbed Mattus's Lowfat Ice Cream, the stuff didn't sell for shit. Have *you* heard of it?

Even More "American" Foods...

ANDOUILLE SAUSAGE
BAVARIAN JELL-O DESSERT
BEEFARONI
BELGIAN WAFFLES
CALIFORNIA ROLL
CHICKEN À LA KING
CHICKEN CACCIATORE
CHILI CON CARNE
CIOPPINO
CLAMS CASINO
CRAB LOUIS
DUTCH BABIES
EGG FOO YOUNG
FAJITAS
FRENCH CRULLER
FRENCH DIP SANDWICH
FRENCH TOAST
FRENCH'S MUSTARD
GERMAN CHOCOLATE CAKE
GUMBO
IRISH COFFEE
JAMBALAYA
LIEDERKRANZ CHEESE
LONDON BROIL
MACHO NACHOS
MEXIMELT
MONTE CRISTO SANDWICH
RAGÚ SAUCE
REUBEN SANDWICH
RICE-A-RONI
RUSSIAN SALAD DRESSING
SALISBURY STEAK
SPAGHETTIOS
SPANISH OMELET
SWISS STEAK
TEQUIZA
WALDORF SALAD

COOL CARS

Baseball, hot dogs, apple pie, and Chevrolet," goes the slogan.

While we didn't invent automobiles, we certainly made 'em better and cheaper. We were the world's first mass producer of cars, and we're the current top producer of cars and trucks (yes, we beat out Japan). It only makes sense that we would've churned out a few classic rides along the way: The Model T, hot rod, "chopped top" lead sled, vintage low-riders, and muscle cars like the Dodge Charger, to name a few.

In addition, the open highway has always been an American metaphor for freedom—the ability to hop in, roll down the windows, crank up the radio, put the pedal to the metal and just drive. Our nation's abundance of gas stations, car washes, drive-ins, drive-thrus, car movies, driving songs, plus over 9,000,000 miles of paved road, all reflect the fact that we love our wheels, whether we're rolling pimp-style in a Caddy, bouncing like fleas in a tricked-out Chevy low-rider, keeping it blue-collar in a pickup, or compensating for something with a 'Vette.

By the way, America *did* invent Big Wheels, Hot Wheels, and bumper cars.

American Rides That Rule!

MODEL T

The first car that was affordable to everyone! Henry Ford introduced his "assembly-line produced" Model T in October 1908. Built at the Piquette Avenue plant in Detroit, it was an instant hit. By 1924, Ford had produced over fifteen million cars with the T engine, dropping the price as low as $290. Beyond the price, what made the T special was its high axles, which allowed drivers to maneuver the crap-laden streets of the horse-and-buggy days. So popular was the Model T that in 1926 they accounted for over half of the world's cars. Still, the T had its limitations. Said Ford: "It's available in any color you want, as long as it's black."

CADILLAC EL DORADO

"Pink Cadillac," "Coupe de Ville," and "Cadillac Ranch"—no ride has been celebrated in song like the Caddy. Their classic American lines, huge fins, and the fact that they are the size of small ships make them the Mack Daddy of motor cars. But Cadillac didn't just sit on those laurels. They also boasted automobile innovations like a distributor, power steering, and three-speed hydromatic automatic transmission! Cadillac is the American status car and remains the leader in the global luxury car market today. Though it's tough to pick a favorite, we'd have to choose the 1959 El Dorado convertible, preferably black.

THE BATMOBILE

If you had a TV show on in the 1960s and needed a car, you didn't call Ford, GM, or Chrysler, you called George Barris, the king of the Hollywood "Kustomizers." George, along with his brother Sam, designed almost every cool car now seen on TV Land. Cars for *Batman, The Beverly Hillbillies, The Munsters,* and *The Green Hornet* all came out of his shop, as well as customized wheels for the likes of Frank Sinatra, Elvis, John Wayne and Steve McQueen. Our favorite is the Batmobile. Essentially a modified 1955 Lincoln Futura concept car, it took Barris three weeks to build and cost $30K. Real fans can see the pre-Bat Futura used in the show in the Debbie Reynolds film *It Started with a Kiss.*

Even More American Cars That Rule...

'31 Chevrolet Coupe/Sedan

'31 Ford Model T Coupe

'32 Ford "Deuce" Coupe

'32 Ford Roadster "High Boy"

'34 Ford Coupe/Sedan Flathead

'40 Ford Coupe 239 Flathead

'49 Mercury Custom "Lead Sled"

'49 Ford Coupe 239 Flathead

'49 Mercury Stock Coupe

'53 Corvette "Blue Flame" 235/160

'55 Chevy Bel Air 265/225 V8

'55 Ford Thunderbird 292 ci

'56 Chevy Bel Air 265 ci

'56 Ford Crown Victoria

'57 Chevy Bel Air 283/220 V8

'57 Ford Thunderbird 312 ci

'57 Corvette 283/283 Fuelie

'58 Chevy Impala 348 Tri-Power

'58 Corvette 283/283 Fuelie

'60 Chevy Impala 348 Tri-power

'63 Corvette Split W 327/360 FI

'64 Ford Fairlane Thunderbolt 427

'64 Pontiac Le Mans GTO 389/360

'65 Mustang 289 (includes 64½)

FUN FACTS

We didn't invent the car, but we did invent:

The first automobile assembly line
(Ford's Model T)

Windshield wipers
(Mary Anderson, 1903)

Car radios
(Paul Galvin's "Motorola," 1929)

Car air-conditioning
(Packard, 1940)

The airbag
(General Motors, 1973)

Cruise control
(blind inventor Ralph Teetor, 1945)

Signaling arm/brake indicator
(silent-film actress Florence Lawrence, 1913)

'69 Corvette L71 427/435

'69 Dodge Charger R/T 440/375

'69 Camaro R/S 396/375

'69 Scooby Doo Mystery Machine

'70 Chevy Chevelle LS6 454/450

'70 Plymouth Hemi
Barricuda 426/425

'70 Buick GSX Stage 1 455/360

'70 Dodge Challenger R/T 426/425

'70 Mustang Boss 302/290

'70 Chevy Chevelle SS 396/375

'70 Olds Cutlass W-30 455/365

'70 Pontiac GTO Judge 455/366

'71 Plymouth Hemi
Barracuda 426/425

'74 Big Foot Monster Truck

Snoop Dogg's Snoop Deville
(coming in 2002)

Even More American Cars That Rule...

'65 Pontiac GTO 389/360 3x2

'66 Shelby AC Cobra 427/425

'67 Corvette 425/435 Tri-power

'67 Camaro SS 396/375

'67 Pontiac GTO 400/360

'67 Shelby Mustang GT-500 428/355

'67 Chevy Chevelle SS 396/375

'68 Corvette 427/435 3x2

'69 Chevy Chevelle SS 396/375

'69 Dodge Charger Hemi 426/425

'69 Camaro Z28 RS/SS 302/300

'69 Mustang Boss 429/375

'69 Pontiac GTO Judge 400/370

'69 Plymouth RoadRunner
440/390 6 pk

FUN FACTS

American Songs About Cars and Driving *(and the folks who sang them)*

"Automobile"—NWA

"Back Seat of My Jeep"—LL Cool J

"Burn Rubber on Me"—Gap Band

"Car Wash"—Rose Royce

"Crosstown Traffic"—Jimi Hendrix

"Cruisin' "—Smokey Robinson

"Diamonds on My Windshield"—Tom Waits

"Drive All Night"—Bruce Springsteen

"Drive On"—Johnny Cash

"Drive South"—John Hiatt

"Greased Lightnin' "—John Travolta

"Hitchhike"—Marvin Gaye

"Hot Rod Lincoln"—Commander Cody

"King of the Road"—Roger Miller

"Little Red Corvette"—Prince

"Mercury Blues"—David Lindley

"My Hooptie"—Sir Mix-a-Lot

"No Particular Place to Go"—Chuck Berry

"Paradise by the Dashboard Light"—Meat Loaf

"Race Car Ya Yas"—Cake

"Rearview Mirror"—Pearl Jam

"Running on Empty"—Jackson Browne

THE WRIGHT BROTHERS

While the concept of flying machines can be traced back to sketches made by Michelangelo, among others, it wasn't until Orville and Wilbur Wright came along that they became a reality. Bicycle mechanics by trade, the Wright brothers elevated their sights to airplanes around the turn of the century. They spent four years tinkering on their farm in Kitty Hawk, North Carolina, before their first successful twelve-second flight in 1903.

The first transcontinental flight took place only eight years later, when Calbraith Rodgers flew from New York to California, crash-landing at least seventy times on his grueling three-day journey.

Now planes crisscross the country at all times of day and night from over 15,000 airports. Air travel has reinvented how the world runs: shuttling executives to and from meetings across the globe, getting fresh Maine lobsters to California while they're still kicking, and sending your mother-in-law back home as fast you can say, "We're *really* sorry you can't stay longer . . ."

VITAL STATS OF THE WRIGHT BROTHERS' FIRST PLANE

CONSTRUCTION: Muslin-covered spruce and ash, powered by a simple four-cylinder engine

WINGSPAN: 40 feet 4 inches

LENGTH: 21 inches

HEIGHT: 9 feet 3 inches

WEIGHT: 605 pounds

Great "High-Flying" Americans

CHARLES LINDBERGH

Piloted by Charles Lindbergh, the *Spirit of St. Louis* was the first plane to be flown nonstop across the Atlantic. In 1927 the *Spirit* flew 3,610 miles from Long Island to Paris in a little over thirty-three hours. When Lindbergh landed in Paris, he became an international hero—and won $25,000 for his efforts. Lindbergh's flight ushered in the era of the airplane as a safe and reliable mode of transportation across long distances. Ostensibly a gas tank with a propeller, the plane was designed by Donald A. Hall, who modified a standard Ryan M-2 for the transatlantic journey. In April 1928, Lindbergh flew the *Spirit of St. Louis* one last time to Washington, D.C., where he gave it to the Smithsonian. What a guy!

CHUCK YEAGER

When you're thinking about pilots with the right stuff, you'd have to put test pilot Chuck Yeager on the top of your list. He was the first guy to break the speed of sound when he flew the Bell X-1 to Mach 1.06 on a clear day in October 1947, flying at a speed of 700 miles per hour at an altitude of 43,000 feet. The plane itself was pretty hip, too. Christened the *Glamorous Glennis* as a tribute to his wife (we guess her name was Glennis), it was the first to feature an adjustable horizontal stabilizer, among other innovations. A die-hard speed junkie, Yeager did over seventy other test flights, going as fast as 957 miles per hour. He won the Purple Heart, Distinguished Flying Cross, Legion of Merit, and other honors. After his high-flying days were over, Yeager went on to write a best-selling autobiography.

Great "High-Flying" Americans

TIMOTHY LEARY

While teaching at Harvard, Leary started the famed Harvard Psilocybin Project, studying the effects of LSD and mushrooms. Hell, sounds like a great job to us! With his famous saying, "Tune in, turn on and drop out," Leary encouraged our nation's college students to eschew their studies and expand their minds by dropping acid. Leary fried with the best of 'em, including Beat writers Allen Ginsberg and Jack Kerouac and famed attorney William Kunstler. In the 1990s, Leary turned his spatial journeys to the cyber world, writing and lecturing on the possibilities of virtual reality. His spirit left this world in '96. His remains followed shortly thereafter when they were launched into outer space, making Leary the highest-flying American of all time.

SHIRLEY MACLAINE

You might know Shirley from her movie career including such famed films as *Being There, The Trouble with Harry, Guarding Tess,* and *The Apartment.* Or perhaps you know her as the sister of Hollywood superstud Warren Beatty. Or maybe you remember her best for her old song-and-dance shit as the female member of the Rat Pack. But she's in this section for her high-flying "out-of-body" experiences. You think you've been there and done that? Well, so does Shirley! A staunch believer in reincarnation as well as astrology, numerology, and UFOs, she's got the balls to write about this foolishness, give plenty of interviews about it, and make a buck on it through her web site, shirleymaclaine.com. She's so ridiculous, she even makes fun of herself in Albert Brooks's movie *Defending Your Life.*

Even More High-Flying Americans...

Kareem Abdul-Jabbar

American bald eagle

Hap Arnold

Colleen Barrett
(COO, Southwest Airlines)

Richard Belzer

Madame Blavatsky

The Blue Angels

Edgar Cayce

Chris Conrad

D. B. Cooper

Bob Denver

Stephen W. Dillon, Esq.

Jimmy Doolittle

Mary Baker Eddy

Barbara Ehrenreich

John Glenn

Woody Harrelson

Ken Kesey

Professor Louis Lasagna
(NORML)

David Lee Roth

Rocket J. Squirrel

REASON 29

HERSHEY BAR

Americans love their candy, from peanut brittle to Jelly Bellies to Pixie Stix. And nothing represents our collective sweet tooth better than the Hershey Bar.

Milton Hershey established his Hershey Chocolate Company in 1894, manufacturing cocoa, baking chocolate, and semi-sweet chocolate. But it wasn't until 1905 that he really hit pay dirt by coming up with his own milk chocolate bar. Did Milt copy anyone else's recipe? Nope! He sat locked in his kitchen until he got the thing right, and thus was born the Hershey Bar. He also helped democratize chocolate via his mass production techniques, price, and quality, making him the "Henry Ford of candy." Hershey's chocolate became a global hit in World Wars I and II, when American soldiers stationed in various countries carried them for quick energy.

American confectioners have also come up with bubble gum, cotton candy, Snickers, Three Musketeers, Tootsie Rolls, Milky Way, Boston Baked Beans, Goobers, Nerdz, Almond Joy, Almond Roca, Mounds, and the York Peppermint Patty. Ah, home sweet home.

SNEAKERS

Every time you throw on your designer running shoes or those comfy, tattered sneakers reserved for weekends, you can say God Bless America.

The Converse "Chuck Taylor" All Star, Nike Air Jordan, Adidas Shell-Toe, and Vans Skate & Surf are all direct descendants of the prototypical footwear created in the nineteenth century by Charles Goodyear (yes, the tire guy).

In 1866, he mixed some sulphur with hot rubber goo, and voilà! Bouncy vulcanized rubber was born. Using vulcanized rubber for the sole and canvas on the top, he created a "croquet sandal" for people who played tennis and croquet. It wasn't long before the trend caught on. They were called sneakers because unlike wood or leather soles, they didn't make any loud click-clack noises, so you could *sneak* around in them.

Each year, our nation spends $2.5 billion on 405.4 million pairs of sneakers, while our own Nike dominates the global market, bringing in just under $9 billion annually ... proof that when it comes to footwear, America kicks ass.

WE GOT GAME

Baseball. Football. Basketball. We invented 'em, we love 'em, and doggonnit, we're great at 'em.

Yeah, we still can't field a soccer team and we generally get our asses kicked in Olympic curling, but sport for sport, Americans definitely *got game*. Golf may have been invented in Scotland, but no one can mess with Tiger. Tennis may have started across the pond, but we'll match Venus Williams against anyone, any day. Europe's got plenty of badass cyclists, but let's not forget our own Lance Armstrong's heroic victories in the Tour de France. And while the Greeks might have come up with wrestling, we've got "athletes" like Stone Cold Steve Austin. We're also pretty adept at surfing, skateboarding, snowboarding, and lots of new, crazy-ass extreme stuff that America invents every other day.

Americans are also experts at sitting on their couches and watching sports, whether it's the World Series, the NBA playoffs, or the Super Bowl.

Great American Sports

BASEBALL

We could simply write up the history of the game—that whole Abner Doubleday thing—but we won't. Baseball is the American pastime, whether we're playing with co-workers, watching it live or on television, or collecting trading cards. It's also great to read about in the morning paper—a baseball junkie can scrutinize player stats like a stockbroker reads the Dow Jones. It's as American as apple pie, and most of us have grown up with it and all its trappings: the hot dogs, Cracker Jacks, Dad drinking beer after beer on a hot day, the smell of freshly cut grass, the crack of the bat, that resolute shout that "He's outta there," and angry demands to "Kill the ump."

FOOTBALL

Some simply dismiss football as an excuse for tons of guys to sit on the couch and drink beer all Sunday, and then do it all again the next night during *MNF*. To that we say: What the hell is wrong with that? American football developed in the nineteenth century from a combination of soccer and rugby, to which we added a healthy dose of American attitude. It's fast, it's fun, and it's furious bone-crushing action. Big guys, hitting other big guys, and they don't even call the cops (unless you're at an Oakland Raiders game). You can keep your scrums and your World Cup and give us the Super Bowl any day.

BASKETBALL

Basketball was invented in Springfield, Massachusetts, in 1891 by James Naismith to entertain athletes at his School for Christian Workers. He used discarded peach baskets for hoops. The game found mainstream acceptance in the 1950s, but it wasn't until Wilt "the Stilt" Chamberlain almost singlehandedly spread the basketball seed to a new breed of fans that b-ball really took off. With superstars like Michael Jordan, Magic Johnson, and Larry Bird, basketball became one of our country's most popular sports. Today Kobe Bryant, Vince Carter, and Allan Iverson are revered like gods. Our favorite is 7'1", 315-pound Shaquille O'Neal, slamming at will and busting rhymes for days. Now, if he could only make a free throw...

American Athletes Who Rule...

Earl Anthony	Mark McGwire
Lance Armstrong	John McEnroe
Arthur Ashe	Dave Mirra
Rocky Balboa	Gorilla Monsoon
Moe Berg	Marc Frank Montoya
Gretchen Bleiler	
Katie Brown	Joe Namath
Nelson Burton Jr.	Ryan Nyquist
Elio Chacone	Bobby Orr
Babe Didrikson	Jesse Owens
Dale Earnhardt	Travis Pastrana
Bobby Fischer	Fritz Peterson and Mike Kekich
Lou Gehrig	
Gorgeous George	Willis Reed
Kerry Getz	Mary Lou Retton
Hank Greenberg	Todd Richards
Tanner Hall	Cal Ripkin Jr.
Dorothy Hamill	Jackie Robinson
Bob Hayes	Sugar Ray Robinson
Tony Hawk	
Roy Hobbs	Bill Russell
Houston	Babe Ruth
Magic Johnson	Sammy Sosa
Kevin Jones	Mark Spitz
Michael Jordan	Y. A. Tittle
Sandy Koufax	Johnny Unitas
Mickey Mantle	Jerry West
Don Maynard	Tiger Woods

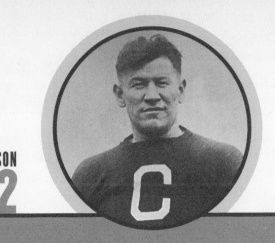

JIM THORPE, ALL-AMERICAN

He's the greatest athlete of the twentieth century, and a shining example of how our great melting pot yields extraordinary individuals capable of extraordinary things. Jim had some French and Irish in him, but he was primarily of Sac and Fox Indian heritage. His birth name, Wa-Tho-Huk, meant "Bright Path," and he certainly lived up to it. He was born in 1887 in a one-room cabin in Oklahoma, but that lack of privilege didn't keep him down.

He won both the pentathlon and decathlon events in the 1912 Olympic Games. That same year, he led his Carlisle Indian School football team to the national collegiate championship, scoring twenty-five touchdowns and 198 points. Following the college football season, Thorpe played six years of major league baseball, while simultaneously leading the Canton Bulldogs football team to unofficial world championships in 1916, 1917, and 1919. He finished his playing days in 1928 with the Chicago Cardinals. Nearly fifty years after his death, ABC's *Wide World of Sports* awarded him their prestigious "Athlete of the Century" distinction.

Jim Thorpe is America at its best.

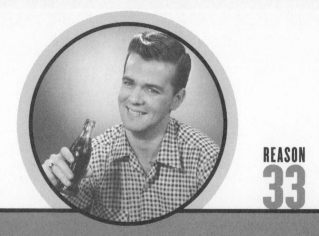

REASON

33

COCA-COLA

What would a hamburger and fries be without a Coke?

Atlanta's Dr. John S. Pemberton invented Coca-Cola in 1886, but it didn't really take off until the company was purchased for $2,300 by Asa Candler. Under Asa, Coke was transformed from soda fountain treat to bottled beverage. Oh, and somewhere along the way, the cocaine used in the original recipe was replaced by caffeine.

Along with being the first bottled soft drink, Coke also pioneered the six-pack, king and family-sized bottles, soft drinks in a can and . . . Santa Claus! Okay, so they didn't give us Santa (Fanta yes, Santa no), but their artist Haddon Sundblom's depiction of the jolly Christmas character became the look of Santa we know today.

For many Americans, the bubbly, caramel-colored drink is like a fifth food group. Every day, 66 million of us have a Coke and a smile, while the world knocks back around 450 million bottles a day. Around the world, Coke is seen as the classic American drink. Ireland has Guinness, Russia has vodka, France has champagne, and Tijuana has tequila poppers, but Coke is what bubbles through our collective veins.

REASON
34

HOLLYWOOD

From matinees to multiplexes, movies are as American as apple pie. We're the epicenter of the business, and we got that big-ass Hollywood sign and the stars on Hollywood Boulevard to prove it. The first person generally credited with using celluloid film for motion pictures was our very own Thomas Edison. Based on his work, the first Kinetoscope parlor—an arcade of peep-show-type machines flashing pix of vaudeville and circus acts—opened in New York City in 1894.

Since then, we've pretty much dominated the market. Other countries make 'em, but ours are the biggest and most popular. The top-grossing movie in history? *Titanic*, grossing almost $2 billion worldwide, or *Gone With the Wind*, which, if released today, would have pulled in almost $4 billion. Top-grossing actor on the planet? Harrison Ford, whose movies have earned over $3 billion.

Cinema verité, mise-en-scène, noir, and all that other arsty-fartsy stuff are cool with us, but nothing beats a good old-fashioned Hollywood blockbuster, and a box of popcorn with artificial butter.

Hollywood Legends

JOHN HUSTON

Son of Walter, father of Angelica, John Huston gained famed as a director, actor, and writer. His directorial debut, *The Maltese Falcon*, was also his first pairing with Humphrey Bogart. Huston would direct Bogart again in such landmark films as *Key Largo, The Treasure of the Sierra Madre* (which starred Dad, who won an Academy Award for his role), and *The African Queen.* And check out his acting chops in *Chinatown*. This guy could do it all! Funny line: After his sanitized autobiography came out a friend supposedly said, "Great book, John, who was it about?"

BOBBY DE NIRO

"You talkin' to me?" From Travis Bickle to young Don Corleone, De Niro is Hollywood's preeminent take-no-shit tough guy. Hard to believe he was the son of two artsy-fartsy New York painters. After a stint in a street gang, he acted off-Broadway and ultimately made the jump to film. With his part as Johnny Boy in 1973's *Mean Streets*, he commenced a long association with director Martin Scorsese, as well as a succession of roles as thugs and gangsters in acclaimed flicks like *The Godfather Part II, Goodfellas*, and *Casino. Taxi Driver, The Deer Hunter*, and *Raging Bull* solidified his tough-guy rep, but he can do funny, too, as illustrated in *Jackie Brown, Wag the Dog, Analyze This*, and *Midnight Run.*

HUMPHREY BOGART

How this short guy with a harelip went on to become *the* movie tough guy is beyond us, but we're down with it. Born in 1899, Bogie landed a series of little go-nowhere movie parts until his breakthrough performance in *The Petrified Forest.* Later teamed with directors John Huston and Howard Hawks, Bogie went on to perform in over fifty films, including *The Maltese Falcon, The Big Sleep*, and *Casablanca.* Married to Lauren Bacall, Bogie held court at his house with all his cronies, leading to the formation of the Rat Pack. By the way, the rumor that Bogie was the original Gerber baby is totally bogus. And while we're debunking urban myth, the Life cereal boy did *not* explode from eating Pop Rocks and drinking a Coke ... so here's looking at you, kid!

American Movies That Rule ...

10
12 Angry Men
101 Dalmatians (animated)
A Nightmare on Elm Street
The Adventures of Buckaroo Bonsai in the 8th Dimension
Airplane!
All About Eve
All That Jazz
All the President's Men
Amadeus
American Beauty
American Graffiti
An American in Paris
Animal Crackers
Animal House
Annie Hall
Antz
The Apartment
Apocalypse Now
Around the World in 80 Days
Attack of the Killer Tomatoes
Ben-Hur
Best in Show
The Best Years of Our Lives
Better Off Dead
Beyond the Valley of the Dolls
Big
The Big Sleep

American Movies That Rule...

Big Trouble in Little China

Bill and Ted's Excellent Adventure

Blacula

Blade Runner

Blood Simple

Blue Velvet

The Blues Brothers

Braveheart

Broadway Danny Rose

Butch Cassidy and the Sundance Kid

Caddyshack

Cape Fear

Casablanca

Cat Ballou

Cavalcade

Chinatown

Citizen Kane

Citizen X

Dances with Wolves

Deep Throat

The Deer Hunter

Debbie Does Dallas

Die Hard

Dirty Harry

Dolemite

Dracula

Duck Soup

Dumb and Dumber

Hollywood Legends

JACK NICHOLSON

The devilish grin. Those arched brows. That naughty charm. Jack's pretty much the coolest actor of his generation, mostly because he's so very good at playing bad. Spending his early career doing B-movies with horror schlockmeister Roger Corman, he made his first real dent in '69 with his role as a boozed-up lawyer in *Easy Rider* with biker buds Peter Fonda and Dennis Hopper. After that, the hits and Oscar nominations just kept coming: *Five Easy Pieces, Chinatown, One Flew Over the Cuckoo's Nest, The Shining, Terms of Endearment, Prizzi's Honor*, and *As Good as It Gets*. He's been just as prolific off camera, fathering loads of kids with various baby mommas.

DUSTIN HOFFMAN

A feisty method actor with a rep for totally absorbing himself in his roles and for telling directors to stick it, Dustin Hoffman spent years in the theater before landing a few small movie roles. His breakthrough came in '67 with *The Graduate*, followed by *Midnight Cowboy*, both of which branded him a counterculture hero. From there, choice parts started rolling in. Starring roles in *Little Big Man, Straw Dogs, Papillon, Lenny, All the President's Men, Marathon Man, Kramer vs. Kramer, Tootsie, Rain Man*, and *Wag the Dog* (we won't mention *Ishtar*) won him tons of praise and awards. Not bad for a short guy with a big honker.

GEORGE LUCAS

Don't let the bad haircut fool ya, it's the only retro thing left from his *American Graffiti* days. The rest is firmly tied into the future of his *Star Wars* saga and his Industrial Light and Magic Company. Born in 1944, the USC Film School grad first made waves with his student film *THX 1138*, but his real place in history came with the 1977 release of *Star Wars*, which rewrote the book not only on what a blockbuster movie was, but how much money you could make selling movie tie-in stuff. With five episodes already in the can, we now wait with bated breath for the final installment. Obi-Wan has taught you well, Master Lucas, though you must've been on crack when you came up with Jar Jar Binks.

Hollywood Legends

HARRISON FORD

A carpenter by backup trade, Ford didn't know if his acting career would ever take off until a little film called *Star Wars* made him a household name. From there Ford went on to star in six of the top thirty all-time grossing movies in Hollywood history! He killed lotsa Nazis in the *Indiana Jones* flicks; stole Kelly McGillis's heart in *Witness*; was the first cybercop in *Blade Runner*; and fought the law in *The Fugitive*. Reluctant action hero, romantic star, able to admit he's scared of snakes—if you don't like Harrison, it's just your own damn fault. Oh, he got that scar on his chin from a car crash when he was twenty-one (back then, he didn't have the dough to see a plastic surgeon).

JULIA ROBERTS

She's only like the biggest female movie star out there! From her humble beginnings as "Eric Roberts's kid sister," she got her big break as "the hooker with a heart of gold" in *Pretty Woman*. Now, the only problem with making such a great flick is finding worthy films to follow it up. She didn't. Witness *Hook, The Pelican Brief*, and *Dying Young*. But then there was that monster comeback. Somehow the scripts got better and Julia was back in bizness with *My Best Friend's Wedding, Notting Hill*, and Oscar-winner *Erin Brockovich*. She's now considered Hollywood gold. Dig this: the $20 million she made for *Erin Brockovich* made her the highest-paid actress of all time! You go, girl!!!

JIMMY STEWART

Could you find a more likable guy? Whether he was talking to a giant rabbit, looking for Zuzu's petals, or peeping through a telescope at a murder in another building, you couldn't help but like this modest everyman just trying to do the right thing. Stewart served in the military in World War II—not as some bullshit song-and-dance guy, but as a bomber pilot. While his association with Frank Capra was a hallmark of his pre-WWII career, so too was his partnership with Alfred Hitchcock after the war. Stewart classics include *It's a Wonderful Life, Mr. Smith Goes to Washington, The Philadelphia Story, Anatomy of a Murder, Rear Window, Rope*, and *Vertigo*.

American Movies That Rule...

Ed Wood

Edward Scissorhands

The Empire Strikes Back

E.T.

Flatliners

Flash Gordon

Flesh Gordon

The Fly

Forrest Gump

Frankenstein

The French Connection

Friday the 13th

From Here to Eternity

The Fugitive

Gandhi

Gentleman's Agreement

Ghostbusters

Gladiator

The Godfather I & II

Going My Way

Gone With the Wind

The Graduate

Grand Hotel

The Great Ziegfeld

The Greatest Show on Earth

The Grifters

Guilty by Suspicion

Halloween

American Movies That Rule...

Hang 'Em High

Harvey

Heavy Metal

High Noon

High Plains Drifter

House of Games

House on Haunted Hill

Indiana Jones I and III
(*Raiders of the Lost Ark* and *Indiana Jones and the Last Crusade*

In the Heat of the Night

Innocent Blood

Invasion of the B Girls

It Happened One Night

It's a Wonderful Life

Jaws

Jurassic Park

King Kong

KISS meets the Phantom of the Park

Kramer vs. Kramer

Lethal Weapon

The Life of Emile Zola

The Lost Weekend

Love and Death

The Maltese Falcon

Manhattan

Marathon Man

Married to the Mob

M*A*S*H

Hollywood Legends

MAE WEST

At a hair shy of five feet in height, Mae West had it all: looks, smarts, a sense of humor, and more moxie than anyone had ever seen up 'til then. For filmgoers during the Depression, Mae's "Why don't you come up and see me sometime?" was the tonic for tough times. Not only did she always look hot and sound horny, but she always had a pithy one-liner ready faster than you can say Jack Armstrong, and was sassy enough to be imprisoned on Roosevelt Island, NY, for indecent exposure. West made only nine movies during her life, but had writing credits for most of them. These movies are generally credited for keeping near-bankrupt Paramount Studios afloat—and made West the highest-paid actress of her time. Our favorite West-ism: "When I'm good I'm very good, but when I'm bad I'm better." Ouch!

BETTE DAVIS

Despite her more recent role as the evil woman in *Return to Witch Mountain*, Bette Davis is considered by most to be one of the greatest actresses of all time. While the rest of her contemporaries were concerned about looking glamorous and making sure that they got the guy in their latest movie, Bette was different. She was less concerned about being a leading lady than she was about landing great roles, which won her multiple Oscars. Choice flix include *All About Eve, What Ever Happened to Baby Jane?, All This and Heaven Too*, and *The Little Foxes*. She never had the looks to kill, but her stare would make you feel like she *could* kill (she really did have Bette Davis eyes!).

JOHN WATERS

"Like a septic tank explosion, it has to be seen to be believed," wrote one paper about *Pink Flamingos*, what many consider John Waters's signature work. It's the one where 350-pound transvestite Divine eats dog poo. Such gratuitous antics are par for the course in Waters flicks, winning him nicknames like "the Prince of Puke" and "the P. T. Barnum of Scatology." Mixing lowbrow humor with 1950s and '60s American kitsch, films like *Mondo Trasho, Polyester* (filmed in "Odorama"), and *Hairspray* (starring

Hollywood Legends

a tubby Ricki Lake) are all cult classics. While his later films boast bigger budgets and less bodily fluids, Waters remains a hero of indie filmmaking.

MEL BROOKS

If you can't sing a few bars of the opening song from *Blazing Saddles*, we bet you can at least hum a few bars of the fart scene! Born and raised in New York, Mel honed his comedic chops on Sid Caesar's *Your Show of Shows* before going on to create some of the funniest movies ever made, including *Blazing Saddles, Young Frankenstein, History of the World Part I*, and *The Producers*. He also produced films like *The Elephant Man* and *My Favorite Year*. He's the king of the lowbrow sight gag, and it's good to be the king.

EDWARD JAMES OLMOS

A movie about a Mexican family or the barrio *without* Edward James Olmos is like a romantic teen comedy without Freddie Prinze Jr.—the dude is ubiquitous. Growing up in East L.A., Ed started off as a rock musician playing gigs on the Sunset Strip, but he really kinda sucked, so he tried acting, and became one of the most respected Mexican Americans in Hollywood. After a series of forgettable parts, he hit pay dirt in the Broadway production of *Zoot Suit*, later reprising his role in the film adaptation. Subsequent credits include *Blade Runner, Mi Familia, Selena*, TV's *Miami Vice* (for which he won an Emmy), and *Stand and Deliver* (for which he got an Oscar nod). But our fave is *American Me*. Olmos directed and starred in this poignant glimpse of Latino gangs, and rumor has it that the Mexican Mafia wasn't too happy with him for doing it. In addition to acting, Olmos is a big humanitarian and activist.

TRACI LORDS

She never won an Oscar, but her performances were Oscar-worthy. That sexy little thing she did with her hair? That alone should've clinched a golden statuette! Traci proved her acting prowess by fooling the entire porn industry into believing she was actually eighteen,

American Movies That Rule...

The Matrix

Meatballs

Midnight Cowboy

Moonstruck

Murder, My Sweet

Mutiny on the Bounty

The Naked Gun

The Natural

Natural Born Killers

New Wave Hookers!

North by Northwest

The Omen

On the Waterfront

One Flew Over the Cuckoo's Nest

Ordinary People

Patton

Plan 9 from Outer Space

Platoon

Psycho

The Producers

Pulp Fiction

Raging Bull

Rain Man

Reefer Madness

Repo Man

Road Trip

Rock and Roll High School

Rocky

American Movies That Rule...

Rushmore

Salvador

Saturday Night Fever

Say Anything

Scary Movie

Schindler's List

Shaft (original)

Shanghai Noon

The Shawshank Redemption

The Shining

Sleeper

The Silence of the Lambs

Snow White and the
Three Stooges

Some Like It Hot

The Sound of Music

Spartacus

Star Wars

The Sting

Stripes

The Stunt Man

Summer Rental

Superfly

Suspect

Swamp Thing

Taxi Driver

The Terminator

Terminator 2: Judgment Day

Hollywood Legends

ultimately costing it millions in recalled videos, and depriving the world of some of the greatest porn *ever*. Born in Ohio, she moved with her family to California at age twelve, and started her movie career at age fifteen. Before authorities discovered her real age, she appeared in tons of hot flicks, including *New Wave Hookers!, Open Up Traci, Sex Fifth Avenue*, and *Beverly Hills Copulator*—now all illegal to own or distribute. While it's hard to think of Traci as anything but a former XXX starlet, we find her efforts to reinvent herself admirable. She has a nice celebrity web site, and an impressive list of credits that don't feature penetration, including *Not of This Earth, Serial Mom, Cry-Baby, Blade*, and TV's *Melrose Place* and *First Wave*. She's also recorded a couple of solid electronic dance albums.

STEVEN SPIELBERG

A master of populist entertainment, this guy is the biggest director in the world. Born in 1946 in Cincinnati and raised in New Jersey, Spielberg was a skinny, unpopular runt as a kid. But he knew how to handle a home movie camera. He lensed the forty-minute war movie *Escape to Nowhere* at age thirteen. At sixteen, his 140-minute film *Firelight* (an inspiration for *Close Encounters*) was shown in a local theater, bringing in a cool $100 at the box office. Spielberg didn't get into film school, but it wasn't long before he was directing movies you never heard of, and TV shows like *Colombo* and *Marcus Welby, M.D.* His big break came in '74 with the release of *Jaws*. Since then, his name has become synonymous with "blockbuster," while his Dream-Works partnership with Jeffrey Katzenberg and David Geffen is kicking Disney's ass.

SPIKE LEE

While many filmmakers just aim to entertain, Spike always manages to make you think, too. From controversial films such as *Do the Right Thing* and *Malcolm X* to the more mainstream *Girl 6* and *Summer of Sam*, Lee's films have helped kick down the doors holding back black filmmakers. Born Sheldon Jackson Lee in Atlanta, he was raised in Brooklyn, and made his first two films, *Last Hustle in Brooklyn* and *Joe's Bed-Stuy Barbershop:*

Hollywood Legends

We Cut Heads, while attending the prestigious Tisch School of the Arts. But it was his *She's Gotta Have It*, about a sexy Brooklyn nympho and her suitors, that first caught Hollywood's attention, winning the Prix de Jeunesse Award at Cannes. Lee also is credited with helping to jump-start the careers of Denzel Washington, Wesley Snipes, Sam Jackson, the Hughes brothers, and others. Be happy the man was born short. Had he been graced with height, the avid Knicks fan may have pursued a career in sports instead of picking up a camera.

JOHN CUSACK

With a mainstream track record *and* indie cred, this Chi-town native has a lower profile than, say, Tom Cruise, but he seems to have a lot more integrity picking roles. If he's in a movie, odds are it's going to be cool and just-left-of-center, even if it's a frothy teen comedy like *Say Anything, The Sure Thing*, or cult classic *Better Off Dead*. He proved his acting chops with serious films like *Eight Men Out* and *The Grifters*; got involved behind the scenes for *Grosse Pointe Blank* and *High Fidelity;* and helped push *Being John Malkovich* to critical acclaim. Between his versatility, his very un-Hollywood 'tude, his off-beat sex symbol status, and an ability to tap into the hipster zeitgeist of the thirtysomething genera-tion, he's our pick for hottest Hollywood up-and-comer.

DREW BARRYMORE

Born in 1975 into a famous acting family that included John and Lionel Barrymore, one of two things was certain: Drew would either be insane or an actress. Well, she had her cake and ate it, too! Though her first role was in *Altered States* at age two, she hit pay dirt as Gertie in *E.T.* While Drew appeared in several other movies, it wasn't until after a cou-ple of stays in rehab that the Drew we all know and love showed up. Drew's movies include *Poison Ivy, Batman Forever, The Wedding Singer, Ever After, Never Been Kissed*, and *Charlie's Angels*. Her production company also kicks ass. We were happy to hear about Drew's recent split with Tom Green, effectively putting her back on the market.

American Movies That Rule . . .

There's Something About Mary
The Thin Man
This Is Spinal Tap
Titanic
To Have and Have Not
Tootsie
Touch of Evil
Toxic Avenger
Toy Story
The Treasure of the Sierra Madre
Two Lane Blacktop
Unforgiven
Up in Smoke
The Usual Suspects
Valley of the Dolls
Victory
Vision Quest
Wayne's World
West Side Story
Wet Hot American Summer
Wild Things
Wings
Witness
The Wizard of Oz
Wizards
X-Men
Xanadu
You Can't Take It with You
Young Frankenstein

ARNOLD SCHWARZENEGGER

Only in America could an immigrant with a hardly pronounceable name, a huge bulky physique, and an accent so thick his first film had to be dubbed become one of the most popular actors on the planet. Of course, we use the term "actor" loosely.

Arnold has never been much for plumbing the recesses of his soul for his various roles. Instead, his calling card is action (*Conan, The Terminator, Total Recall, The Running Man, Predator, True Lies*) and witty one-liners, delivered in a broken Austrian accent with uneven cadences in his voice, flip-flopping W's to V's and P's to B's. Phrases like "I'll be back" and "Hasta la vista, baby!" are permanently etched in our consciousness.

The best part about Arnold is that he makes no bones about being some sort of great method actor, regularly poking fun at his own action-packed career. And while some of his recent films kinda tanked (what were they called?), we're fairly certain *T3* will put him back on the map.

FUN FACTS

Six things you might not know about Ahhhnold:

1. To get him his first movie role in *Hercules Goes to New York*, Arnold's body-building mentor Joe Weider told the film's producers that Arnold had been a Shakespearean actor in England.

2. In *The Terminator*, the part of the nefarious cyborg almost went to real-life villain O. J. Simpson.

3. Before he started acting, Arnold received a degree in Business & Economics from the University of Wisconsin, invested winnings from his body-building competitions in real estate and a mail-order body-builder equipment company, and became a millionaire before age twenty-two.

4. A staunch Republican, Arnold is married to longtime Democrat Maria Shriver, a member of the Kennedy clan.

5. Before coming to America, Arnold had three dreams: to win Mr. Olympia, to marry a Kennedy, and to become President. Two outta three ain't bad, but he's threatened to run for political office sometime in the future.

6. His nickname is "the Austrian Oak." We can't confirm whether that's above or below the belt.

FUN FACTS

What's Poppin', America?

1. Popcorn, a native Indian dish, was enjoyed by the Pilgrims at the first Thanksgiving!

2. Americans consume 17.3 billion quarts of popped popcorn each year (that's approximately 1.12 billion pounds)!

3. The average American eats about 68 quarts of popcorn each year—or 55 trash cans full over a lifetime!

TIMES SQUARE

Imagine December 31st without the ball dropping. Without Times Square, where would Dick Clark spend his New Year's Rockin' Eve? And where would we be without the "zipper sign," which has informed New Yorkers of everything from V. E. Day to JFK's assassination to the winner of last night's Yankees game?

When the *New York Times* moved its office to a new twenty-five-story skyscraper at Broadway and 42nd Street in 1904, Longacre Square officially became known as Times Square. Since then, the rectangle of streets bordered by Seventh Avenue, Broadway, 42nd, and 48th has been both the shining center of the city as well as its blighted core.

Forty-Deuce's giant billboards have blown Camel smoke rings; poured brimming glasses of Coca-Cola; and featured oversized images of everyone from the Beatles to Linda Lovelace. The fans who once swooned over Frank Sinatra at the Palace on 47th and Broadway now scream for *NSYNC on MTV's *TRL* at 44th and Broadway. Times Square is both a piece of history and the modern pulse of one of the world's greatest cities.

And for those of you looking for the hookers, Rudy moved them to Jersey.

MARRIAGE

"I do."

Words of lifelong commitment are uttered more times in the U.S. than in any other nation in the world—including those nations permitting multiple marriages. It's estimated that every year, 2,000,000 American couples get hitched. As of 2000, it was estimated that 57,000,000 folks were husband and wife.

It's not just about the numbers, either. In America, you have the right to marry whoever the hell you want, provided they're of age (even in Alabama). The number of mixed marriages in our country—1,400,000—is proof of this freedom. And there's no limit (Elizabeth Taylor and Mickey Rooney are testament to this fact). Finally, you can make your vows how and where you want, whether it's in a big frilly ballroom, under water, under a giant two-story tiki head, on TV, or at a drive-thru chapel in Vegas. It's a pretty simple process—just a state-issued license, maybe a blood test, and the consent of two adults. Perks include cool tax benefits and free gifts!

We recommend registering at Bloomingdale's, Williams-Sonoma, or theweddingchannel.com.

DIVORCE

"Parting is such sweet sorrow."

Not for everyone. Some people can't untie the knot fast enough. Fortunately, in America, it's no big deal. Hell, it's practically a national pastime. Around two million divorces are granted each year, and 10 percent of all American adults are divorcés.

While severing the bonds of matrimony may not be cause to celebrate, the ease with which you can do it certainly is. The government can't say no, and most states have "no-fault" divorce laws. Another convenient option is annulment—it's like that shit never even happened.

Don't like that no-good, deadbeat, couch-potato rat bastard? Divorce his ass! Out with the old, in with the new, no nasty stigma attached. Just hire a lawyer to do the dirty work.

HARLEY-DAVIDSON

The wind in your face. Gas fumes tickling your nostrils. That distinct (and trademarked!) *"potato potato potato"* sound rumbling in your ears. And 700 pounds of quivering steel, aluminum-magnesium, and rubber between your legs.

We didn't invent the motorcycle, but we certainly came up with the world's coolest thing on two wheels. For decades, Harley-Davidson has been a symbol of rebellion, freedom, the promise of the open road ... and America in general. Japanese bikes may be faster and more precise, but when it comes to cruising down the highway and looking for adventure, Harley is the unchallenged king of the road.

HD's patented V-Twin motor takes its cue from the engine that William Harley and Walter Davidson connected to a carburetor made from empty tomato paste cans in a Milwaukee shed at the turn of the century. By 1917, production had reached 18,000 bikes a year.

One hundred years later, Harley-Davidson is not just a set of wheels, but an entire culture, with sales in the millions, and thousands upon thousands of loyal "bro's" who swear allegiance to the black and orange.

ROUTE 66

Stretching 2,400 miles between Chicago and L.A., it's more than a highway. It's a straight-up slice of Americana, tar-and-asphalt-style.

Started in 1926 and finished in '38, the diagonally configured road aimed to connect small towns to a major national thoroughfare, thereby linking hundreds of rural communities and allowing farmers to transport their wares efficiently. Stamped the "Mother Road" by John Steinbeck in his novel *The Grapes of Wrath*, it also allowed thousands of Americans to escape the hopelessness and, well, dustiness of the Dust Bowl and head west. For many, it was indeed the road to opportunity.

The highway also gave rise to prototypical service stations, motels, diners, goofy tourist traps, and other roadside businesses that are emblematic of America's car and road trip culture. Connecting lush green forest to high desert to low desert, and rife with lore, it's a metaphor for the joys, possibilities, and mystery of the open road.

FUN FACTS

Emergency Route

The song "(Get Your Kicks on) Route 66" was written by Bobby Troup, who also played a doctor on the 1970s television show *Emergency!*

LAS VEGAS

Strippers. Gambling. Hookers. Booze. Palatial hotels. Mob lore. All-you-can-eat shrimp. What more could you want? Sure, you lose a crapload at the tables, but you make up for it at the buffet.

Sin City is more than just a place. It's a symbol of decadence and debauchery known the world over—a giant adult Disneyland where ass, flash, and cash are all readily available. They've also got some great shows, four-star restaurants, and a really big dam, but who cares about that?! You come to Vegas to party hard, double-down, and maybe even get married by Elvis at a drive-through chapel.

The Mormons who first settled in Vegas in 1855 had no idea that their sleepy desert town would someday be host to over thirty million visitors a year, with annual Nevada gaming revenues surpassing $8 billion.

OURS IS BIGGER . . .

*The MGM Grand is the biggest hotel in the world,
covering 112 acres, housing 5,005 rooms,
a 15,200-seat arena, and a 33-acre theme park.*

REASON
42

THE RAT PACK

They epitomized cool, had attitude to spare, and could find a drink, a smoke and a broad anywhere, 24/7. They were the Rat Pack.

While their name was derived from the "original" Holmby Hills Rat Pack of Humphrey Bogart, Lauren Bacall, Frank Sinatra, Judy Garland, Sid Luft, Swifty Lazar, Jimmy Van Heusen, David Niven, and Kay Thompson, the incarnation we know and love included Frank as the Chairman of the Board, and board members Dean Martin, Sammy Davis Jr., Peter Lawford, and Joey Bishop.

Their mission was simple, said Sinatra: "We're not setting out to make *Hamlet* or *Gone With the Wind*. The idea is to hang out together, find fun with the broads, and have a great time. We gotta make pictures that people enjoy. Entertainment, period."

And that's what they did throughout the 1960s. Their nightclub shtick at the Sands was legendary (along with their after-hours carousing). Cool to this day, nobody got away with more crap than these guys. And while their movies weren't *Hamlet, Ocean's Eleven* and *Robin and the Seven Hoods* sure were fun as hell!

Meet the Rats

FRANK SINATRA

The Chairman of the Board, Sinatra was head Rat for several reasons. First, he was the biggest star, with hit songs, hit movies, hot chicks, et al. Plus... Frank *reputedly* knew how to make "problems" disappear faster than you can say "Luca Brazzi." Francis Albert Sinatra was born in 1915 in Hoboken, New Jersey, to Italian immigrant parents. After being discovered in 1939, Sinatra became the ultimate crooner for the Tommy Dorsey band—Ol' Blue Eyes was the first singer to really make girls swoon and faint. He starred in lots of great movies as well as lots of bad movies, and was a legend among legends. And if he didn't bang a broad, she clearly wasn't worth banging!

SAMMY DAVIS JR.

Amidst the racial divides of the 1950s, being a short, skinny, black, one-eyed, Jewish Republican married to a white chick wasn't exactly a recipe for success. Yet Sammy not only succeeded, he flourished. One of a kind, he was the consummate song-and-dance man, with a voice that could be heard two states away. Davis, a charter member of the Rat Pack, had tons of hit songs including "The Candy Man," "That Old Black Magic," and our favorite, "The Theme from *Baretta*." He appeared in numerous movies, and his book *Yes I Can* was an international bestseller. Can you dig it, baby?!

DEAN MARTIN

The ultimate straight man to Jerry Lewis, as well as the ultimate cool Rat, Dean Martin (born Dino Paul Crocetti) was a boxer, crooner, comic, and TV and movie star. What separated Dean from the Pack was that he just didn't give a shit. Drink and smoke firmly in place, he cruised through the Vegas nightlife, seemingly without effort or a care in the world. To Dino, everything was *all good*. And did ya know that his TV shows in the 1960s and '70s made him so much loot that he was the largest shareholder of NBC? His song "Everybody Loves Somebody" also knocked the Beatles off the top of the charts in 1964.

Frank Sinatra Songs That Rule...

"A Fine Romance"
"All or Nothing at All"
"Chicago"
"Come Fly with Me"
"Come Rain or Come Shine"
"Embraceable You"
"Fly Me to the Moon"
"Hey Jealous Lover"
"High Hopes"
"I Get a Kick Out of You"
"It Was a Very Good Year"
"I've Got a Crush on You"
"I've Got You Under My Skin"
"The Lady Is a Tramp"
"Luck Be a Lady"
"Misty"
"My Blue Heaven"
"My Way"
"New York, New York"
"Night and Day"
"One for My Baby"
"South of the Border"
"Stardust"
"Strangers in the Night"
"Summer Wind"
"Tangerine"
"That Old Black Magic"
"That's Life"
"Three Coins in the Fountain"
"Witchcraft"
"Young at Heart"

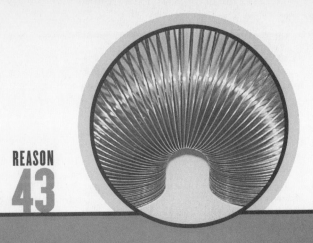

THE SLINKY

Are we a fun country, or what?!

From childhood, we're blessed with one of our nation's greatest resources: cool toys and games. We didn't invent chess, but that's complicated and boring, while Chinese Checkers is just plain boring. We'd rather play Monopoly, Clue, or pinball any day! America also invented the Frisbee, Barbie, Hot Wheels, and, of course, the Slinky.

Who doesn't love a Slinky? America's paradigmatic unisex toy, it's fun for a girl and a boy! Plus, it walks down stairs, alone or in pairs, and makes a slinkity sound. Finally, it's affordable to all and easy to operate, no batteries or assembly required. Unlike some modern toys, you don't need to be a rocket scientist to put it together or play with it.

Ironically, the spring-like novelty item was invented by a scientist, or at least a naval engineer. In 1943, Richard James was trying to develop an anti-vibration device for ship instruments. But once he saw the way his invention walked down shelves, he came up with a new plan, and took it to Gimbel's department store. At $1 per unit, Gimbel's sold out the original 400 Slinkys, and a fad was born.

America at Play

TWISTER

When the Milton Bradley Company released this "social interaction" game in 1966, they feared that consumers might not go for a game without the traditional board and pieces. They were also worried about the flack they might get for selling what competitors were calling "sex in a box." But as they say, sex sells. Once Twister was featured on *The Tonight Show*, with guest Eva Gabor in a low-cut gown on all fours and Johnny climbing on top of her, sales went through the roof—three million games in the first year alone! To date, over 65 million people around the world have played this silly excuse to get physical, ranging from pint-sized kiddies to drunk, naked adults.

BARBIE

90% of all American girls in the last forty years have owned a Barbie, and if every Barbie ever made were laid end-to-end, they would circle the earth three and a half times! (Of course, Barbie can't *really* get laid, since Ken has no genitalia.) The ultimate "babe in Toyland" made her debut in New York in 1959. Mattel founders Ruth and Elliot Handle named the twelve-inch brunette in a black-and-white bathing suit after their daughter. Over the years, she's changed with the times, and worn clothing designed by everyone from Christian Dior to Bob Mackie. She's no bubblehead, either, counting veterinarian, doctor, and astronaut among her many careers. At age forty-two, she's still pretty hot. If she were human, it's estimated her measurements would be 39-21-33!

SPIN THE BOTTLE

You can't buy it at Toys "Я" Us, but it's amused generations of American youth as much as any doll or board game, don't you think?! Plus, it's free. All that's needed is a bottle and three or four pairs of lips. Invented by horny preteens at a slumber party, or at summer camp, or wherever parents were not to be found, the game can be naughty or downright nasty, depending on the age and daring of the players. More mature American kissing games include Truth or Dare, Seven Minutes in Heaven, and Seven Minutes in Hell.

More American Toys That Rule...

Action Jackson
Battleship
Boggle
Clue
Crayola crayons
Crossword puzzles
Easy Bake oven
Erector set
Etch-A-Sketch
Frisbee
G. I. Joe
Hot Wheels
Lincoln Logs
Lite-Brite
Madame Alexander dolls
Magic 8-Ball
Mr. Potato Head
Operation
Ouija Board
Pictionary
Pogo Stick
Raggedy Ann & Andy
Rock'em Sock'em Robots
Scrabble
Sea Monkeys
Shrinky Dinks
Silly Putty
Sorry
Taboo
Tinker Toys
Tonka trucks
Toy trains
Transformers
Trivial Pursuit
View-Master
Yahtzee!

TELEVISION

The Brits, Swedes, Germans, and French all had a hand in the various inventions that led to modern TV as we know it, but it was Philo T. Farnsworth, a graduate of Utah's Brigham Young University, who developed the "dissector tube," the basis of all current electronic televisions, in 1927. More importantly, America's Zenith Corporation invented the first TV remote in 1950, and couch potatoes across America are forever in its debt.

In addition, we've come up with the world's best and most popular shows. Folks in far-off lands know all about the voyages of the various *Enterprise* crews, or what fashion-savvy Rachel is wearing on *Friends*.

Finally, we're proud to say that we're some of the best TV watchers on the planet. In 1939, when TV broadcasting started in the United States, there were only 400 TV sets. By 1953, 50 percent of American homes had one; by 1974, that number had risen to 97 percent. Today, the average American watches over four hours of quality programming every single day.

As to the idea that watching TV kills brain cells—fuck it, you've got millions of those suckers to spare.

American TV Shows That Rule!

THE SOPRANOS

Fuhgetaboutit. The best friggin' show on TV, it's *Ozzie and Harriet in Hell*, or *Godfather Knows Best*. Only in America could a mob killer become a sympathetic character. His problems are your problems: not getting enough dough from the rackets, those nosy Feds, sell-out snitches, the proper disposal of bodies. You root for Tony to make breakthroughs with his therapist so he can sleep better at night and get rid of those pesky panic attacks. And yes, you cried when Big Pussy went to sleep with the fishes.

I LOVE LUCY

"Loooo-cy, I'm home!" Since its 1951 debut, over a billion people have tuned in to the antics of that crazy redhead and her babaloo-ing hubby. Unable to find a sponsor, husband-and-wife team Desi Arnaz and Lucille Ball used their own dough for a pilot. CBS picked it up, filming in front of a live audience with three separate cameras, a major innovation that became the blueprint for future sitcoms. The couple started making $30,000 a week; five years later, they made $350,000 per episode, which today equates to $1 million per episode. It was the top-rated show for four seasons, and was followed by a number of popular Lucy spinoffs. Now in syndication, it's probably the most watched show ever.

LAW & ORDER

We just can't get enough of this show—which is good, since it seems like it's on all the time. One part cops, one part lawyers, it's today's version of *Dragnet*, only without all of Joe Friday's funny walking. *L&O* first started airing in 1990, with each show following the half-and-half formula and featuring storylines "ripped from today's headlines." Now, 12 years later, it's the longest-running drama out there. While cast members have come and gone, the show's quality has remained, though we must admit we do miss grumpy DA Adam Schiff and his ever-present hat.

Even More American Shows That Rule...

A-Team
Adam 12
The Addams Family
Alice
All in the Family
American Bandstand
America's Most Wanted
The Andy Griffith Show
Angel
Barney Miller
Batman
Batman Beyond
Battle of the Network Stars
Battlestar Galactica
Baywatch
Bewitched
The Beverly Hillbillies
Beverly Hills 90210
The Big Valley
The Bionic Woman
The Bob Newhart Show
Bonanza
The Brady Bunch
The Bugaloos
The Bullwinkle Show
Captain Kangaroo
Charlie's Angels
Cheers
Chico and the Man
CHiPs
Colin's Sleazy Friends
Columbo
Combat!
Cops
The Courtship of Eddie's Father
Dallas
Days of Our Lives

Even More American Shows That Rule...

American TV Shows That Rule!

YOUR SHOW OF SHOWS

Imagine you're Sid Caesar, it's 1950, and NBC asks you to create a sketch comedy program for television. You look for some young hungry writers— a few kids who can make you laugh a bit—and you end up with a gag writer's Hall of Fame: Mel Brooks, Woody Allen, Neil Simon, Larry Gelbart, Carl Reiner. Their wild, over-the-top humor—subversive and trippy years before anyone used drugs—was the inspiration for future TV landmarks including *Get Smart, Saturday Night Live, David Letterman*, and *Pee-Wee's Playhouse*. Interesting tidbit: Sid Caesar once beat up Mel Brooks while arguing over a joke, taking the concept of "physical comedy" to a whole new level.

SATURDAY NIGHT LIVE

We dare you to think of another television show that has produced more shtick and one-liners: "Cheezzzburger, cheezzburger," "Jane, you ignorant slut," "I'm Gumby, dammit," "Never mind," "Land shark." And the list goes on. *SNL* first aired on October 11, 1975, with the classic cast of Dan Aykroyd, John Belushi, Chevy Chase, Jane Curtin, Garrett Morris, Laraine Newman, and Gilda Radner. Later alums include Bill Murray, Eddie Murphy, and Billy Crystal. With cutting-edge humor, great musical guests, and biting political satire, *SNL* is funny *most* of the time. *SNL* is also famous for producing some of the funniest (and worst) movies of all time.

SEINFELD

From 1990 to 1998, Jerry, Kramer, George, Elaine, and characters like the Soup Nazi and Bubble Boy made us laugh about the minutiae of everyday life. Nothing was sacred: Jerry and crew made fun of everyone (the hearing-impaired, ugly people), and then laughed their asses off to the bank. Jerry made $267 million in 1998, making him the world's best-paid actor EVER, while *Seinfeld* co-

American TV Shows That Rule!

writer Larry David earned $242 million that year, making him the best-paid TV writer EVER—ironic considering that NBC originally passed on the series. Thirty million weekly viewers made it a Top Five Nielsen show for six straight years, and through reruns, it's still one of the top sitcoms in syndication. Not bad for a show about nothing.

SOUTH PARK

Who would ever have thought that a bunch of burping, farting, potty-mouthed tykes would take the TV 'toon world by storm? Cartman, Stan, Kenny, and Kyle grabbed the baton from Beavis and Butt-Head and ran with it, transforming Comedy Central's low-budget animated series into an international phenom. University of Colorado film students Matt Stone and Trey Parker first made a short cartoon called *Jesus vs. Frosty* featuring the future South Park characters. The Fox network loved it, and paid them to make another short to be sent to celebrities as a Christmas card. The response was so great that a series was inevitable. Some parents don't find the show appropriate viewing for kids. Our advice? Blame Canada.

60 MINUTES

Since 1968, that ticking stopwatch has symbolized no-holds-barred investigative reporting on our nation's top issues. Every Sunday, an average of 17.1 million viewers tune in to see who or what Mike Wallace and crew are going to expose, from health care organizations to corrupt government officials. Indeed, when Mike shows up at your door, you know you're fucked. (We won't mention that minor transgression with tobacco companies.) For twenty-three consecutive seasons, the newsmagazine show has ranked among Nielsen's top ten highest-rated prime-time programs, a record that no other program can touch. Incidentally, the first stopwatch—they've used a bunch of 'em—is on display at the Smithsonian.

Even More American Shows That Rule...

Jeopardy!
The Jetsons
Kukla, Fran and Ollie
Kung Fu
Knight Rider
Land of the Lost
The Larry Sanders Show
Lassie
Late Show with David Letterman
Laverne and Shirley
Leave It to Beaver
Lidsville
Little House on the Prairie
The Lone Ranger
Lost in Space
Love, American Style
The Love Boat
Magnum, P.I.
The Man from U.N.C.L.E.
Mannix
Married with Children
The Mary Tyler Moore Show
McHale's Navy
M*A*S*H
Match Game
Maverick
Melrose Place
The Merv Griffin Show
The Milton Berle Show
Mission: Impossible
The Mod Squad
Monday Night Football
Moonlighting
Mr. Ed
The Munsters
My Favorite Martian
Nanny and the Professor

Even More American Shows That Rule...

The Newlywed Game

Night Gallery

The Odd Couple

Ozzie and Harriet

The Partridge Family

Perry Mason

Planet of the Apes

Police Squad!

The Price Is Right

Quincy, M.E.

Rawhide

The Rifleman

The Robin Byrd Show

The Rockford Files

Route 66

Scooby-Doo!

The Simpsons

The Six Million Dollar Man

Smallville

Son of the Beach

Soul Train

The Soupy Sales Show

SportsCenter

Star Trek

Starsky and Hutch

Superman

Survivor

SWAT

Talk Soup

Taxi

That's Incredible

Three's Company

American TV Shows That Rule!

IN LIVING COLOR

Politically correct? Homey don't play that. Remember laughing your ass off at sketches like "Homeboy Shopping Network," "Handi-Man," "Fire Marshal Bill," and the *Star Trek* spoof, "The Wrath of Farrakhan"? Though it only ran four and a half years and never made it into the Top 30, this multira-cial variety show helped establish a struggling Fox network by boldly going where *Saturday Night Live* wouldn't dare. Fusing a strong African-American point of view, biting commentary, hysterical com-edy, and live hip-hop, *In Living Color* was one of the most cutting-edge shows of its time. It also intro-duced us to the Wayans Brothers, Jamie Foxx, Jim Carrey, and David Alan Grier, while J-Lo and Rosie Perez both started off as *ILC* "fly girls."

The Tonight Show

TJ Hooker

Twenty-One

Twilight Zone

Twin Peaks

Vegas

VIP

The Virginian

Wait Till Your Father Gets Home

Wagon Train

Welcome Back Kotter

What's Happening

Wheel of Fortune

The White Shadow

Wild Kingdom

The Wild Wild West

WKRP in Cincinnati

Wonderama

Wonder Woman

The Wonder Years

The X Files

Xena: Warrior Princess

THE FENDER STRATOCASTER

It was in the 1950s that Leo Fender first introduced the solid-body electric guitar called the Esquire, which begot the Broadcaster, which begot the Telecaster, which evolved into the Stratocaster, got that? Over fifty years later, the Fender line of guitars (and Fender electric basses) are the world standards.

Fenders have a style and sound all their own. They're beautiful, they're simple, and in the right hands (hell, even in just so-so hands) they can rock like a mother! Chances are the discs in your CD changer were recorded using one. Here's a list of axslingers who swear or swore by their Strats: Jimi Hendrix, Stevie Ray Vaughan, Eric Clapton, Kurt Cobain, Billy Corgan, Merle Haggard, Bob Mould, Bob Dylan, Dick Dale, Bonnie Raitt, David Gilmour, Eric Johnson, Jeff Beck, Muddy Waters . . . we could go on and on.

The true test of the Fender Stratocaster's greatness? Close your eyes and picture what an electric guitar looks like. It's a Strat.

ROCK 'N' ROLL

You can keep your oom-pa-pas and opera and give us some of that ol' time rock 'n' roll! We challenge you to name a "popular" style of music not invented in the United States. Blues, rock, jazz, country, metal, rap, disco, techno, house, and punk all have their roots firmly planted in U.S. soil.

From Robert Johnson's twelve-bar delta blues to Elvis's gyrations to the Ramones' "Gaba Gaba Hey" to Eminem's lyrical wizardry, nobody has rocked harder or created more music than us.

Where would the Beatles be without Chuck Berry, Little Richard, or the King? Our sounds rule the worldwide airwaves. We can't knock Mozart, but you sure as shit can't get jiggy to him!

These Rock Stars Rule!

JAMES BROWN

It's no wonder he felt like being a sex machine. Born into a poor backwoods Georgia family, James went to live at his aunt's brothel at age five. His sordid past also includes drug addiction, robbery, a high-speed car chase, illegal possession of firearms, and assault. The only thing longer than his rap sheet is his hit list: "Papa's Got a Brand New Bag," "I Got You (I Feel Good)," "Say It Loud—I'm Black and I'm Proud," to name a few. "The Godfather of Soul" was also known for his piercing screams, flying splits, and one-legged skates. In the past fifteen years, his songs have enjoyed new life as hip-hop artists pilfer his shrieks and his beats.

BOB DYLAN

We can't say enough about this moody guy who you can't understand when he speaks and sorta understand when he sings. But hey, read the lyrics, and they're pretty damn great. Born Robert Zimmerman in Duluth, Minnesota, Dylan changed his name, hit the road, and started writing great folk songs like "The Times They Are a-Changin'," "Blowin' in the Wind," and "Mr. Tambourine Man." When he put down his acoustic guitar and picked up an electric, he changed rock 'n' roll forever, instilling a depth in the music that no one had even come close to. Start with "Highway 61" and work your way through the collection.

SUGAR HILL GANG

Sylvia Robinson, co-owner of New Jersey's Sugar Hill Records, heard an underground tape recorded at a party, where guys were rhyming to a beat, and she decided it was time to cash in on the trend. She started assembling a group with Wonder Mike and Master Gee. When she heard club bouncer Big Bank Hank "rapping" at a pizza joint near her house, she knew she'd found the third member. Backed by Chic's "Good Times," SHG's "Rapper's Delight" stormed the charts in 1979. There were plenty of rappers and DJs before them, performing at parks and parties, and there most certainly were far better rappers after them. In fact, it's even disputed whether or not the group actually penned the song's lyrics ("Hotel, motel, Holiday Inn . . ."). But theirs was the first commercial rap single *ever*, paving the way for

Even More American Rockers Who Rule...

Cannonball Adderly

Aerosmith

Dave Alvin

The Archies

Erykah Badu

Chet Baker

The Beach Boys

The Beastie Boys

Bobby "Blue" Bland

The Blasters

Blondie

The Blues Brothers

Gary "U.S." Bonds

Booker T. and the M.G.'s

Bon Jovi

Charles Brown

Ruth Brown

Roy Buchanan

Buckwheat Zydeco

R. L. Burnside

The Byrds

David Byrne

The Cars

Tracy Chapman

Ray Charles

Cheap Trick

Patsy Cline

Eddie Cochran

John Coltrane

Nat "King" Cole

Sam Cooke

Aaron Copland

Even More American Rockers Who Rule...

The Cramps

Creedence Clearwater Revival

Marshall Crenshaw

Crosby, Stills and Nash

Christopher Cross

King Curtis

D'Angelo

Dick Dale

Bobby Darin

The Dead Kennedys

De La Soul

Bo Diddley

Ani DiFranco

Dion

Willie Dixon

Fats Domino

The Doors

Dr. Dre

The Drifters

Steve Earle

Earth, Wind & Fire

Duane Eddy

Ramblin' Jack Elliot

Joe Ely

Eminem

EPMD

Eric B & Rakim

Firehose

The Four Seasons

The Four Tops

Doug E. Fresh

Robbie Fulks

These Rock Stars Rule!

the "conscience" rap of Public Enemy, the gangsta rap of NWA, punky white boys like Eminem, and even the rap-rock of Limp Bizkit.

LOUIS ARMSTRONG

Considered by many to be the father of jazz, Louis Armstrong was born in New Orleans in 1900 and blew his way to the top...okay, he played the trumpet, but man, could he blow! Armstrong is credited with melting the New Orleans Tin Pan Alley sound with traditional blues and a heavy dose of improvisation. He had tons of hit songs as a band leader and singer, and later led his own Louis Armstrong Quartet. Armstrong is also credited with creating "scat"—improvised vocal bebops. The story goes that Armstrong forgot the lyrics to a song and just started to "scat" made-up words to go with the melody. In that sense, some historians credit him as the world's first rapper.

LOS LOBOS

Los Lobos (The Wolves) were not *Just Another Band from East L.A.*, as their first album's title suggested. Garfield High School friends David Hidalgo, Cesar Rosas, Louie Perez, and Conrad Lozano originally played from a repertoire of 150 traditional Mexican songs, until a fateful gig when they opened for John Lydon's band PIL. Fusing punk attitude, roots-rock, rockabilly, and traditional Mexican music, Los Lobos went on to carve their own niche in pop, appealing to punk rockers and the NPR crowd alike. Choice albums include *How Will the Wolf Survive, Kiko,* and *The Neighborhood.* Ironically, their rendition of "La Bamba" reached #1 on the *Billboard* charts, while the original only made it up to #22.

KISS

You couldn't really rock 'n' roll all night and party every day until these masked musical avengers came on the scene with such ferocious hits as "Black Diamond," "Detroit Rock City," "Calling Doctor Love," and the ballad "Beth." For three decades, Paul Stanley, Gene Simmons, Ace Frehley, and Peter Criss have preached the gospel that rock should be ear-splitting, obnoxious, ridiculous, and fun as hell! Not content to just make music and have tons of

These Rock Stars Rule!

groupie sex (just listen to songs like "Plaster Caster"), Kiss, Inc. has made sure that *every* member of their "Kiss Army" has plenty of Kiss merch to keep them happy from the cradle (Baby Kiss stuff) to the grave (the new Kiss coffin). Raise your Bic lighters in the air!

BRITNEY SPEARS

She may only have fifteen minutes, but damn if she isn't making the most of them. The Louisiana native started off on *The Mickey Mouse Club*, but her big break came in 1998 with the release of *Baby, One More Time*, followed by two other discs that collectively sold millions upon millions of records worldwide. Even if you think her stuff is sonic pablum (look it up), you gotta admit that the chick can sing and dance...and her tight tight ass doesn't hurt, either. No, *Oops...I Did It Again* will not go down in history as an example of classic songwriting, but it's a great example of glossy, infectious American pop. Bouncy blonde Britney is the quintessential American teen superstar.

BILLIE HOLIDAY

Born in Baltimore in 1915, Eleanora Fagan Gough adopted the name of her father (her folks never married), a minor jazz guitarist named Clarence Holiday. We don't know where the "Billie" came from. Even today, she remains the paradigmatic haunted jazz singer, living the old line, "If she didn't have bad luck, she'd have no luck at all." Too much booze, too many drugs, smokes, and bad men. But Holiday took all of that shitty luck and infused her songs with it, letting listeners literally feel her pain. Choice cuts include "Strange Fruit," "Lover Man," and "Don't Explain." Her melancholic style has influenced too many singers to name.

MILES DAVIS

Between his hair extensions, temperamental nature, and proclivity for playing with his back to his audience, trumpeter Miles Davis was a kooky cat, but a cool one nonetheless. After his foray into bebop, he laid down the blueprint for the West Coast "cool jazz" style with *Birth of the Cool*, and for jazz

Even More American Rockers Who Rule...

Milt Gabler
Marvin Gaye
Dizzy Gillespie
Philip Glass
The Go-Gos
Grandmaster Flash and the Furious Five
The Grateful Dead
Al Green
Green Day
Woody Guthrie
Merle Haggard
Bill Haley and the Comets
John Hammond
Slim Harpo
Emmylou Harris
The Reverend Horton Heat
Buddy Holly
John Lee Hooker
Hüsker Dü
Ice Cube
Ice T
Ice Tray
The Isley Brothers
The Jackson Five
Janet Jackson
Mahalia Jackson
James Jamerson
Elmore James
Etta James
Jane's Addiction
Jefferson Airplane
Joan Jett

Even More American Rockers Who Rule...

Jewel

Billy Joel

Little Willie John

Freedy Johnston

Janis Joplin

Louis Jordan

Josie and the Pussycats

Jurassic Five

Kid Rock

Albert King

B. B. King

Kool and the Gang

Lenny Kravitz

Cyndi Lauper

Leadbelly

Jerry Lee Lewis

Limp Bizkit

Linkin Park

Little Richard

LL Cool J

Professor Longhair

Lyle Lovett

Frankie Lymon
and the Teenagers

Curtis Mayfield

MC5

The Minutemen

Missing Persons

Bill Monroe

The Moonglows

Jelly Roll Morton

The Motels

Mötley Crüe

fusion with *Bitches Brew*. Such chameleon-like style changeups stamped him with the nickname "The Picasso of Jazz." Over a fifty-year career, he scored countless Grammy awards and nominations, and played with everyone from Dizzy Gillespie, Charlie Parker, and John Coltrane to Herbie Hancock, Chick Corea, and Quincy Jones. The dude was prolific; like Tupac and Hendrix, albums featuring newly resurfaced Miles performances pop up every year.

2 LIVE CREW

Long before the courtroom scuffles of P-Diddy, Jay-Z, Eminem, Snoop, and ODB, the Crew fought the law...and won. Formed in the mid-80s by Luke Campbell, AKA Luke Skyywalker, they made headlines when their album, *Nasty as They Wanna Be*—featuring "The Fuck Shop," "Head Booty and Cock," and "Me So Horny"—was banned as obscene by the state of Florida. The band was then arrested for performing the record's songs in concert. Everyone from the ACLU to Bruce Springsteen rushed to their defense, screaming freedom of speech. The Crew ultimately triumphed, but Luke had to drop the *Star Wars* reference in his stage name when George Lucas sued him, and he paid heavily when the makers of the movie *Full Metal Jacket* sued over the unlicensed sample of dialogue in "Me So Horny." He evened his win-loss ratio when the Supreme Court ruled that the Crew's version of Roy Orbison's "Oh, Pretty Woman" was parody, *not* copyright infringement. Luke also gets props for being the first black owner of an independent hip-hop label, and for getting blown onstage by cute Japanese fans.

THE MONKEES

Never mind *NSYNC, The Backstreet Boys, Milli Vanilli and Eden's Crush, give it up for the Monkees. A cheap knockoff of the Beatles' *A Hard Day's Night*, the "Prefab Four" was a band manufactured for television, but ultimately became a legitimate fad of their own. After over 400 candidates were auditioned, Mike Nesmith, Peter Tork, Mickey Dolenz, and Brit Davy Jones were chosen. With songs penned by ringers like the famed writing team of Tommy Boyce & Bobby Hart ("I'm Not Your Steppin' Stone," "Last Train to Clarksville," "Daydream Believer"), as well as Neil Diamond ("I'm a

These Rock Stars Rule!

Believer"), the Monkees were sure to come up with a few hits. Amazingly, in 1966 the band went on to sell more records than the Beatles and the Rolling Stones! Indeed, Monkee business had become big business. When the fame faded, the boys took a decade off, and reemerged as the paradigmatic retro act. By the way, the answer to your burning questions are "yes" and "yes": Mike Nesmith's mom did invent Liquid Paper, and a then unknown Jack Nicholson did co-write the script to the Monkees' film *Head* in 1968.

HANK WILLIAMS

"Hey good lookin', whatcha got cookin'?" is just one of the famous lines written by Hank Williams. In his short, whiskey-drinkin', drug-takin', womanizing, no-good life, Hank managed to pen some of the greatest country songs ever written. These songs include "Your Cheatin' Heart," "I'm So Lonesome I Could Cry" and "I'm a Long Gone Daddy." As opposed to those who died young and left a good-looking corpse, Williams died at the age of twenty-nine, but looked like he was sixty. He is also directly responsible for producing Hank Williams Jr., whose "All My Rowdy Friends Are Coming Over for Monday Night Football" we could really do without.

JIMI HENDRIX

Just when you think you know how to really rock out, Jimi Hendrix comes along and starts changing the rules with his guitar "voodoo." While we're really not sure what planet he was from, he did some shit with his guitar that people are still scratching their heads about. Rife with psychedelia, Hendrix's songs mixed hard rock, blues, jazz, and pyrotechnics when other guys were content to just play loud. His best work includes "Purple Haze," "Hey Joe," and "All Along the Watchtower." Hendrix's rendition of the "Star-Spangled Banner" at Woodstock is also considered a rock landmark. Rock on, voodoo chile!

GEORGE CLINTON

One Nation Under God? How 'bout "One Nation Under a Groove"! Armed with his famous "Bop Gun" and a fusion of R&B and hard rock, George "Dr. Funkenstein" Clinton and his various configurations of funkateers (Parliament, Funkadelic,

Even More American Rockers Who Rule...

Bob Mould

Willie Nelson

New York Dolls

Notorious B.I.G.

N.W.A.

Roy Orbison

Outkast

Charlie Parker

Van Dyke Parks

Gram Parsons

The Partridge Family

Les Paul

Pearl Jam

Tom Petty & the Heartbreakers

The Pixies

The Plimsouls

Doc Pomus

Elvis Presley

The Pretenders

Prince

Public Enemy

Ma Rainey

Bonnie Raitt

Lou Rawls

Otis Redding

Jimmy Reed

R.E.M.

The Replacements

Smokey Robinson

Jimmie Rodgers

Rollins Band

The Roots

Even More American Rockers Who Rule...

- Sam and Dave
- Del Shannon
- The Shirelles
- The Silver Platters
- Simon and Garfunkel
- Slick Rick
- Sly and the Family Stone
- Smashing Pumpkins
- Jimmy Smith
- Snoop Dogg
- Sonny & Cher
- Spahn Ranch
- Sparks
- Spinal Tap
- Staind
- Steely Dan
- Strawberry Alarm Clock
- The Stray Cats
- Suicidal Tendencies
- Sun Ra
- The Supremes
- The Talking Heads
- Television
- The Temptations
- Texas Tornados
- They Might Be Giants
- Tom Tom Club
- Allen Toussaint
- Tower of Power
- A Tribe Called Quest
- Tupac
- Big Joe Turner

These Rock Stars Rule!

P-Funk All-Stars) sought to invigorate all zones of zero funkativity, freeing too many booties to count. Hidden amid all the bouncing bass, nonsensical sci-fi-speak, and crazy costumes was sharp social commentary about government oppression and being black in America. Today, Clinton continues to record and sell out shows, while rappers regularly sample his funked-up jams.

ARETHA FRANKLIN

We love her *despite* her crazy hair and odd fashion sense. Before Aretha, most black singers were relegated to doo-wop, sappy ballads, and jazz numbers. Aretha changed all of that. "Lady Soul" started her recording career back in 1960, and gained a strong black following, but it wasn't until 1967 that the hit song "Respect" catapulted her to mainstream fame. Today, she has over twenty million-selling singles to her credit, and her huge voice *still* towers over any backup band, no matter how loud they are. Next time you watch *The Blues Brothers*, look for her scene-stealing song and dance number, "Think."

BRUCE SPRINGSTEEN

Bruuuccceee! Okay, so the Springsteen worship thing is a little too much for us. On the other hand, he wrote songs that captured the American zeitgeist better than anyone else ever has. With "Born to Run," "Thunder Road," "Atlantic City," and too many others to name, Springsteen told stories about everything from love, hope, and longing to pink Cadillacs and the open road. Backed by the E Street Band's New Jersey sound, Bruce is also legendary for his live shows, which have been known to stretch as long as four hours. By the way, Steve Van Zandt, Springsteen's longtime guitar player, now represents a different side of New Jersey as Silvio Dante on *The Sopranos*.

BESSIE SMITH

What Louis Armstrong is to Miles Davis, Bessie Smith is to Billie Holiday. Born on April 15, 1894, in Chattanooga, Tennessee, she is considered the most influential female blues singer of her time. Known as "the Queen of All Torch Singers," she's famous for her recordings of " 'Ain't Nobody's Bizness if I Do,"

These Rock Stars Rule!

"Nobody Knows You When You're Down and Out," and "After You've Gone." Our favorite Bessie Smith story is that before a gig, she heard that there were some KKK freaks outside her tent. Bessie busted outside and shouted, "You just pick up them sheets and run!" They ran. You just don't mess with Bess.

JOHNNY CASH

You can take your cowboy-hat-wearing, mid-tempo corporate country music and shove it! Give us Cash! Always cool, never out of style, the quintessential "Man in Black," Cash is the outlaw's out-law. He's been there, done that with basically everything: drugs, booze, broads...you name it. And like the ancient hero who descends into hell only to come out stronger, Johnny has always delivered the goods after his misdeeds, including songs like "Ring of Fire," "I Walk the Line," and "Folsom Prison Blues." Here's a Cash tidbit: his hit "A Boy Named Sue" was actually penned by Shel Silverstein, author of the kid's book *Where the Sidewalk Ends*.

ROBERT JOHNSON

So the story goes that one day, a young Mississippi guitarist—filled with a burning desire to play the blues—went down to the crossroads to make a deal with the devil. That's the legend of Robert Johnson, the master of the delta blues. No one's really sure about much more about the man: who he was, or how he really died. Stories abound of him being poisoned by a jealous woman, or frothing at the mouth on all fours like a dog as the devil was cashing in on his contract. What we do know is that in his short, tormented life, Johnson recorded songs that are considered the heart and soul of the blues: "Crossroads," "Sweet Home Chicago," and "Love in Vain."

CHUCK BERRY

In 1955, Chuck Berry released "Maybel-lene" and made rock history. Like the famous shot heard 'round the world, this white crossover hit was the seed from which the mighty tree of rock 'n' roll would grow. In a segregated America, Berry's music simply appealed to every kid; he was the most popular artist of any race, period. Over the next few years, he continued to write hit songs that would become

Even More American Rockers Who Rule...

Tina Turner
Twisted Sister
Ugly Duckling
Townes Van Zandt
Stevie Ray Vaughan
Ritchie Valens
Van Halen
The Velvet Underground
The Ventures
Gene Vincent
Loudon Wainwright III
Tom Waits
Was (Not Was)
T-Bone Walker
Dinah Washington
Muddy Waters
Barry White
White Zombie
Chris Whitley
Wilco
Lucinda Williams
Bob Wills
and His Texas Playboys
Jackie Wilson
Johnny Winter
Howlin' Wolf
Stevie Wonder
X
Weird Al Yankovic
Yeastie Girls
Frank Zappa
John Zorn

These Rock Stars Rule!

eternal rock mainstays such as "Johnny B. Goode," "Roll Over Beethoven," and "C. C. Rider." Here's something you may not know: while Berry continues to tour, he hires each band in the cities he's playing (they just need to know his greatest hits), and insists on being paid in cash before each performance.

THE RAMONES

Considered by many to be the founding fathers of punk rock, The Ramones were formed by four high school friends in 1974 with a mission to produce the greatest music ever known... okay, they had no mission. As a matter of fact, they really had no musical talent, either. But in the land of opportunity, pure adrenaline is enough. The band quickly jelled, and within two years of playing fast, fun, and furious three-chord songs at New York's famed CBGB's, this leather-clad crew released their first album, *Ramones*, to a hungry audience. Their legacy includes "(I Wanna Be) Sedated," "Rock 'n' Roll High School," and "Blitzkrieg Bop." Kinda makes you wanna go sniff some glue, don't it?!

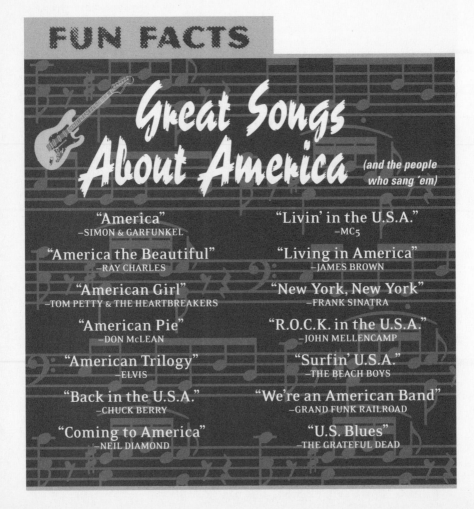

FUN FACTS

Great Songs About America *(and the people who sang 'em)*

"America"
–SIMON & GARFUNKEL

"America the Beautiful"
–RAY CHARLES

"American Girl"
–TOM PETTY & THE HEARTBREAKERS

"American Pie"
–DON McLEAN

"American Trilogy"
–ELVIS

"Back in the U.S.A."
–CHUCK BERRY

"Coming to America"
–NEIL DIAMOND

"Livin' in the U.S.A."
–MC5

"Living in America"
–JAMES BROWN

"New York, New York"
–FRANK SINATRA

"R.O.C.K. in the U.S.A."
–JOHN MELLENCAMP

"Surfin' U.S.A."
–THE BEACH BOYS

"We're an American Band"
–GRAND FUNK RAILROAD

"U.S. Blues"
–THE GRATEFUL DEAD

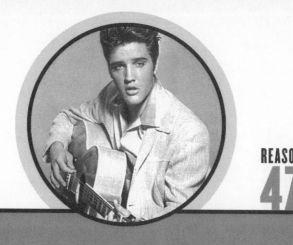

ELVIS

Well, he didn't really invent rock 'n' roll, but he did popularize it. The pork-chop-sideburned "hunka hunka burning love" also popularized the pelvic thrust and the peanut butter and banana sandwich.

Elvis was born in 1935 in Mississippi to poor, religious parents who later moved to Memphis, Tennessee. Becoming a truck driver after high school, one day he passed a studio with a sign advertising "MAKE YOUR OWN RECORDS." As a gift for his mom, he recorded "That's When Your Heartache Begins" in a "rockabilly" style that fused his country roots with black R&B. Hits like "That's All Right, Mama" and "Heartbreak Hotel" followed, and the rest is history. In his lifetime, he sold 300 million albums and made thirty-three movies, while his bold, sexy style has influenced nearly every rock singer since.

Since his "supposed" overdose in 1977, "the King" has been elevated from mere legend to god. He lives on in the form of continued record sales, ceramic busts, crushed velvet portraits, vials of toenail clippings, scores of impersonators, and tabloid headlines. Today he ranks as the most sighted dead celebrity on the planet.

DEAD
CELEBRITIES

Other countries have martyrs. We've got dead celebrities. Elvis. Marilyn. Jimi. Tupac. These are the stars who lived hard and died young—stars who either burned too bright too fast, or who met with sudden, legend-making tragedy.

Whether they OD'ed, shot themselves, drove off a cliff, died in a plane crash, or drowned in their own vomit, these icons have become larger than life—pop culture gods worshiped for decades after their death.

But are they really dead? No other country in the world has had more of its supposedly dead celebs abducted by aliens, or hiding out somewhere on a remote tropical island.

Other "Dead" Celebs!

BRUCE LEE

Born in San Francisco in the Year of the Dragon (that would be 1940), Lee was badly beaten up at age thirteen. So he took up martial arts and became a chop-socky legend, paving the way for the likes of Jackie and Jet. At age thirty-three, on the set of *Game of Death*, Lee went to go lie down—and never got up. While doctors ruled his demise "death by misadventure," it's widely believed it was the result of a cerebral edema. But as they say, the show must go on. Bruce Lee movies and merch remain popular the world over. Tragically, his son, Brandon, followed in his fatal footsteps when a prop gun misfired during the filming of *The Crow*.

JIM MORRISON

Did he die of heart failure in a bathtub in France, or is he living in Africa under the name Mojo Rising? Lots of mystery surrounds the death of Jim Morrison. There was never an autopsy performed, yada yada yada. What's really important here is that the legacy lives on. Every year a new group of hippie youth discover the Lizard King for the first time, get high, and buy Doors and Morrison gear by the ton. He lived the ultimate life of sex, drugs, and rock 'n' roll, with a dash of art and poetry thrown in. Chicks dug him, and guys wanted to be him (because chicks dug him). He's the ultimate rock martyr.

AMELIA EARHART

Like the existence of Bigfoot, space aliens, and the lost city of Atlantis, the disappearance of this famed aviator remains one of America's greatest enduring mysteries. The first woman to fly solo across the Atlantic while establishing a new transatlantic record, Earhart was celebrated throughout the world and received a medal from President Hoover. A few years later, she also became the first woman to successfully fly from Hawaii to California. But it was her final flight in 1937 that ensured her place in Dead Celebrity History. As she attempted to fly around the world, her plane vanished without a trace somewhere between New Guinea and Howland Island. Spooky!

Even More Great American Dead Celebrities...

AALIYAH
DUANE ALLMAN
JOHN BELUSHI
THE BIG BOPPER
JEFF BUCKLEY
TIM BUCKLEY
PATSY CLINE
KURT COBAIN
BOB CRANE
JAMES DEAN
CHRIS FARLEY
JUDY GARLAND
PHIL HARTMAN
RITA HAYWORTH
JIMI HENDRIX
BUDDY HOLLY
HARRY HOUDINI
JANIS JOPLIN
ANDY KAUFMAN
JOHN F. KENNEDY
JOHN F. KENNEDY JR.
ROBERT F. KENNEDY
JAYNE MANSFIELD
SAL MINEO
MARILYN MONROE
RICKY NELSON
HEATHER O'ROURKE
RIVER PHOENIX
DANA PLATO
JACKSON POLLOCK
ELVIS PRESLEY
OTIS REDDING
RANDY RHODES
SAVANNA
SELENA
TUPAC SHAKUR
NANCY SPUNGEN
BIGGIE SMALLS
RITCHIE VALENS
ANDY WARHOL
NATALIE WOOD
MARIAH CAREY (CAREER DEAD)

REASON
49

SUPERMAN

True, he's faster than a speeding bullet, and more powerful than a locomotive. He can fly through space, hear things miles away, and see through pretty gals' dresses. But more importantly, he's a first-generation immigrant, rocketing millions of miles through space from Krypton to Smallville, U.S.A., where he grew up to fight for truth, justice, and the American way.

Talk about a prime example of our great melting pot!

The world's first superhero was created in the 1930s by two nerdy, bespectacled teens. More Clark Kent than men of steel, they probably couldn't get laid to save their lives. Which is a good thing, since they devoted all their efforts to creating Superman. After countless rejections, he finally soared onto the pages of 1938's *Action Comics* #1. An instant hit, Superman was soon picked up as a daily newspaper strip, followed by radio, TV, movies, and even Broadway. A truly universal icon known across the earth, the blue-and-red-caped hero has also appeared on products ranging from puzzles to peanut butter.

Superman's success paved the way for other American safeguards of justice, including Batman, Aquaman, Spider-Man, Wonder Woman, The Hulk, Captain America, and Super Chicken.

FUN FACTS

Super-Pricey!

The world's most valuable comic book is a 1938 first edition of *Action Comics* #1, featuring the first appearance of Superman. The thirteen pages of Superman's adventures in that issue focused on unjust imprisonment, spousal abuse, and corrupt government officials. In 1997, it sold for $100,000.

DISNEYLAND

Once American kids learn to talk, the second place they demand to go, after McDonald's, is Disneyland.

Parents rarely agree that it's "the happiest place on earth." The lines can be hell, the heat sweltering, and by the time you're done with parking, admission, concessions, and mouse ears, you practically need to take out a second mortgage on your house. But most of us have fond memories about a childhood trip to the Magic Kingdom, whether it's getting lost for hours on Tom Sawyer's Island, screaming in terror on the Matterhorn, making Mom lose her lunch on the spinning tea cups . . . or doing a bid in the infamous Disneyland Jail.

The park opened in 1955 on a day remembered as "Black Sunday." Tickets to a VIP grand opening party were counterfeited; the big steamboat nearly capsized; it was over 100 degrees; water fountains didn't work; and Main Street's asphalt was still gooey. But that didn't stop Disneyland and its sister parks in Florida, Tokyo, and France from becoming the four most visited amusement parks on the planet, with a grand total of 68,000,000 visitors in 2000 alone.

Some of them are still waiting in line.

THE PILLSBURY DOUGHBOY

Sell sell sell, buy buy buy. It's the American way, and an integral part of this process is the great art of advertising. In order to lure consumers (and their kids) into buying all sorts of junk they don't really need, U.S. marketing minds have come up with some of the most clever and enduring advertising icons on the planet.

Our all-time favorite—and one of the most renowned in history—is the Poppin' Fresh Doughboy.

In 1960, the Leo Burnett ad agency needed a memorable character to instruct consumers how to make Pillsbury's heat-and-eat "Poppin' Fresh" dough. Their answer came in the form of a doughy white little spokesperson in a baker's hat, bow tie, and no pants. Voiceover actor Paul Frees (also the voice of Boris from *The Bullwinkle Show*) added the final touch: a patented giggle now recognized by millions across the globe.

DID YA KNOW...?

Barry Manilow wrote the McDonald's jingle "You Deserve a Break Today."

Even More American Pitch Men & Women...

AUNT JEMIMA

BETTY CROCKER

BOB'S BIG BOY

BUSTER BROWN

CAP'N CRUNCH

CHEF BOYARDEE

CHIQUITA BANANA

COLONEL SANDERS

COPPERTONE GIRL

COUNT CHOCULA

DUTCH BOY PAINTS

ELSIE THE COW

GEOFFREY THE GIRAFFE

JUAN VALDEZ

JULIO & MARISOL

THE MARLBORO MAN

THE MICHELIN MAN

MR. KLEEN

MR. PEANUT

MR. WHIPPLE

MRS. OLSON

THE NOID

OLD CROW

THE QUAKER GUY

RONALD MCDONALD

ROSIE THE RIVETER

THE SLIM JIM GUY

SMOKEY THE BEAR

SNUGGLE BEAR

SPUDS MACKENZIE

THE TACO BELL CHIHUAHUA

THE TY-D-BOL MAN

THE TRIX RABBIT

TOUCAN SAM

TROJAN MAN

Other American Ad Icons That Rule!

JOLLY GREEN GIANT

Ho, ho, ho! The big green fella in the leaf loincloth pushed Green Giant canned veggies on us for years. He made his debut in 1925 as the spokesperson for their peas, but gradually came to be the symbol for the whole company. He didn't say much, but was known for his trademark laugh. In the 1960s, he adopted a mischievous little sidekick named Sprout to help him sell his wares, forming a sales team that made rival vegetable companies green with envy. Today the Green Giant sells everything from sweet corn niblets to diced veggie medley in Asia, Canada, Greece, and throughout the Middle East. He's also honored with a fifty-five-foot Green Giant statue that greets visitors entering Blue Earth, Minnesota.

GERBER BABY

Oh, baby! In the early 1920s, an overworked mom asked her hubby, Dan Gerber, if his canning company could possibly puree some peas for their baby daughter. And with that, the baby food industry was conceived. Their trademark was a charcoal sketch of the perfect baby, which was later replaced by a photo version of the perfect baby. Today, that chubby-cheeked face graces everything from Gerber baby charm bracelets to mugs. And the Gerber baby food company? They're still at it, providing strained peas, applesauce, summer medleys, and fancy mushed-up chicken to toothless kiddies across the globe. And for the discerning baby, they even have a new line of organic food.

ENERGIZER BUNNY

Like America itself (or a guy on Viagra), he just keeps going and going and going. Since 1989, the pink, battery-powered bunny in shades and blue sandals has been banging on that drum. To date, the hearty hare has popped up unexpectedly in 115 TV commercials, and has taken home multiple advertising awards. He's easily among the top ad icons of the twentieth century. He's been spoofed in a number of films. And he's currently honored with an entire online store of Energizer Bunny plush toys and apparel, and a Hot Hare Balloon that stands 166 feet tall—fifteen

Other American Ad Icons That Rule!

feet taller than the Statue of Liberty, with ears as tall as the presidents' faces on Mount Rushmore!

TONY THE TIGER

Thank your lucky charms that when Kellogg ran a contest in the 1950s to choose their new spokesbeast for Frosted Flakes, kids didn't pick Katy the Kangaroo, Elmo the Elephant, or Newt the Gnu! The original Tony the T made his breakfast debut in 1953, claiming that Frosted Flakes not only tasted good, but "Grrreat!" Another brainchild of legendary ad man Leo Burnett, Tony evolved from a prim and proper pussy with well-coifed whiskers into the cool, colorful cat we know today. And if you think his voice sounds familiar, you'rrrrrre right! Tony voiceover Thurl Ravenscroft was also the voice of numerous critters in Disneyland (listen for him in the Haunted Mansion), and belted out "You're a Mean One, Mr. Grinch" in the original animated adaptation of *Dr. Seuss' How the Grinch Stole Christmas.*

THE CRYING INDIAN

Iron Eyes Cody appeared in almost 90 movies and numerous TV shows, but he is most widely remembered for this role as the "crying Indian." If you grew up in the 1970s and watched the tube, you know what we're talkin' about. Standing in stark contrast to Woodsy the Owl's cutesy "Give a Hoot, Don't Pollute" campaign, the "crying Indian" commercials were launched in 1971 on the first-ever Earth Day. The ads featured Native American Iron Eyes Cody walking and canoeing through polluted American landscapes, a single teardrop rolling down his cheek. His heart-tugging plea for ecology struck such a nerve that it was recently voted one of the top fifty advertising campaigns of all time.

BLEACHMAN

Superheroes have always been about justice, saving lives, and doing the right thing. Gotham City's in trouble? Get Batman! Lex Luthor's back in Metropolis? Call Superman! Junkies in San Francisco dying of AIDS? You need Bleachman! In an effort to help curb AIDS transmission from infected nee-

American Slogans That Rule...

"A little dab will do you."

"Bammm!"

"Built Ford tough."

"Celebrate the moments of your life."

"Do the Dew."

"Do you tip a hooker?"

"Don't leave home without it."

"Eat me."

"Flick of the Bic, sir?"

"Friends don't let friends drive drunk."

"Good to the last drop."

"Got milk?"

"Ho! Ho! Ho!"

"I'm Jennifer, fly me!"

"It's not just a job, it's an adventure."

"Just Do It."

"King of beers."

"Let your fingers do the walking."

"Like a rock."

"Loose lips sink ships."

"M'm! M'm! Good!"

"Pardon me, do you have any Grey Poupon?"

"Please don't squeeze the Charmin!"

"Plop plop, fizz fizz."

"Reach out and touch someone."

American Slogans That Rule . . .

"Ribbed, for her pleasure."

"Silly rabbit, Trix are for kids!"

"Strong enough for a man,
but made for a woman."

"Takes a lickin', but keeps
on tickin.' "

"Tastes great! Less filling!"

"Think different."

"We will sell no wine
before its time."

"Where's the beef?"

"You sunk my battleship!"

"You've got mail."

". . . But wait, there's more!"

Other American Ad Icons That Rule!

dles, the San Francisco AIDS Foundation started the controversial superhero ad campaign in 1988. Like his superhero brethren, Bleachman had a cape, wore his underwear on the outside, and protected the underclasses. Unlike his counterparts, he hung out with spikeheads and preached, "Clean It with Bleach." We don't advocate shooting up or wearing underwear outside your tights (or wearing tights in general), but we're all about saving lives.

FUN FACTS

Any Way You Slice It . . .

Okay, so we didn't invent sliced bread, but we did invent the automatic bread slicing machine! Otto Rohwedder first exhibited his invention in 1928. Just five years later, automatic bread slicers were slicing 80 percent of the bread sold in the U.S.!!!

REASON
52

THE SMITHSONIAN

Want to see Archie Bunker's chair, Abe Lincoln's top hat, and fossilized pterodactyl feces, all in one place? Check out the Smithsonian. The custodians of Americana, they separate the priceless crap from the rest of the crap.

Established in 1846 by James Smithson, Washington, D.C.'s Smithsonian Institute consists of sixteen museums and galleries, the national zoo, and tons of research facilities that house a whopping 140 million pieces. Smithsonian museums include: the National Air and Space Museum (planes from the Wright Brothers, all sorts of space capsules), the National Museum of Natural History (dinosaur stuff), the National Portrait Gallery (famous pictures of Washington as well as regular Renaissance-type art), and the National Museum of American History (Fonzie's jacket, Kermit the Frog).

Not to bag on the Louvre, but unlike other stuffy museums, the Smithsonian is fun and kid-friendly. Plus it's FREE. We recommend getting really baked, putting on your Walkman, and walking through the National Portrait Gallery. It's a hoot, and you'll feel like you're being cultural.

HOT SHOWERS

Ever travel outside the U.S.? If so, the first thing you probably notice—after the bidet—is that you can't always count on that plentiful hot water streaming out of your tap.

In America, a hot shower in the morning is practically a God-given right. Set the shower controls to full blast, soap up, and watch yesterday's dirt and grime swirl down the drain.

Every day of the year, Americans use three billion gallons of water to shower. If cleanliness is next to godliness . . . well, you get the idea.

DID YA KNOW...?

When the average American showers, he or she spends twelve minutes under the spigot, and 45.2 percent of us admit to peeing in the shower (the rest just lie about it).

FUN FACTS

Country Fresh!

In addition to being some of the most frequent bathers in the world, Americans invented the following items to keep things nice and clean . . .

★ The Q-Tip
★ Deodorant (roll-on and aerosol)
★ Tampons
★ Ty-D-Bol

THE USDA

Thanks to these guys, you can bite into a juicy burger with the knowledge and comfort that it's not going to kill you ... at least not right away.

The United States Department of Agriculture worries about the quality of meat, poultry, eggs, vegetables, and canned and frozen products so you don't have to. More than 7,600 personnel verify that regulations regarding food safety, and other consumer protection concerns such as labeling, are met in nearly 6,500 meat, poultry, and egg processing plants.

In 2000, we ate 46,000,000,000 pounds of red meat and 30,000,000,000 of poultry ... all blessed with the approval of one of the most advanced and efficient food inspection systems on the planet. You just can't beat our meat.

FUN FACTS

Fire It Up!

While the idea of putting meat over fire and having a barbecue isn't an American invention, it was the combined efforts of Henry Ford and Thomas Edison that gave us the first charcoal briquette!

MARTIN LUTHER KING JR.

Other countries have their royal families, but America has its Kings. Not those who ascended to leadership by some fluke of birth, mind you, but those who did so by the content of their character.

And no one had finer content of character than Martin Luther King Jr. Like Gandhi before him, King showed the world that peaceful demonstration and civil disobedience were a righteous path toward political change.

A Baptist minister by trade, King was born in 1929 in Atlanta, Georgia. When he accepted his first pastorate at the Dexter Avenue Baptist Church in Alabama, so started his mission as a civil rights leader. With landmark rallies and demonstrations like his 1963 March on Washington, King helped open the eyes of a segregated country. In 1964, he was rewarded for his efforts with a Nobel Peace Prize. On April 4, 1968, those efforts led to his assassination in Memphis, Tennessee, by James Earl Ray.

Today, he is revered for his courage, while his immortal words, "I have a dream...," continue to inspire the eradication of social injustice in any form.

More Great American Kings

B. B. KING

Born Riley B. King in Mississippi in 1925, the nickname Blues Boy or B. B. is how he's known to the world. Armed with a black Gibson guitar named Lucille, King has been playing his version of the blues from sea to shining sea for almost sixty years. On classics like "The Thrill Is Gone," "Why I Sing the Blues," and "When Love Comes to Town," it's King's economical style that sets him apart from the pack. Not a wasted note; if it's not there, it wasn't meant to be there. He's a poet who can condense an entire emotion into a single riff.

BILLIE JEAN KING

Considered the greatest female tennis player of her time (if not the greatest athlete), Billie Jean was the first woman to make over $100,000 in prize money in any sport. Her tennis accomplishments include six Wimbledon singles victories and numerous U.S. championships. She was also captain of our Olympic tennis team in 1996 and 2000. As a women's rights pioneer she was also a champ, arguing for equal treatment and payment for women in sports. When famous sexist tennis pro Bobby Riggs said that no woman could defeat him, King took the challenge, and beat the pants off him 6-4, 6-3, 6-3 in front of a capacity crowd at the Houston Astrodome in 1973.

DON KING

Only in America could a guy with that hair rise to the top of his profession. The ultimate fight promotor and hypemaster, King set up some of the world's greatest fights, including the famed "Rumble in the Jungle" Ali-Forman bout and the first Mike Tyson–Evander Holyfield match, which shattered all previous pay-per-view records. His fights have generated anywhere between hundreds of millions and a billion dollars in revenues, and he was the first promoter to guarantee $1 million paydays to nonheavyweights. Almost equal to his ringside accomplishments are his contributions to the English language—King has an uncanny ability to make the simplest statement sound like a thrillified immensification of epical verbalosity.

More American Royalty...

Albert King
Budweiser (King of Beers)
Burger King
Butterfly McQueen
Carole King
Coretta Scott King
Crown Royale
Duke Ellington
Duke Robillard
Duke Snider
The Dukes of Hazzard
Earl Schieb
Elvis Presley (The King)
The Fresh Prince of Bel Air
John Wayne (The Duke)
King Cobra
King Kong
King Kong Bundy
King Vidor
King Taco
King Tee
King of All Media
(See Howard Stern)
King of Pop
(What's left of Michael Jackson)
Larry King
Nat "King" Cole
Patty Duke
Prince
Prince Charming
Prince Paul
Princess Grace of Monaco
Queen Latifah
Queen for a Day
Stephen King
Steve McQueen

MEDICINE

As problem solvers, the U.S. reigns supreme. Got a leaky faucet? We can fix it. Having trouble with that clutch? Let's take a look at it. That same "we can fix it" attitude applies to our approach to medicine. American medical innovations led us out of the dark ages of leeches and bloodletting, and into a multibillion-dollar industry of leeches and bloodletting!

Americans have pioneered everything from cures for athlete's foot to open-heart surgery to the X-ray machine. We've stopped polio, eradicated smallpox, cured cholera, and helped sculpt the bodies of your favorite Playboy Bunnies. And while we haven't cured everything (including the common cold), our doctors have been at the forefront of research and treatment for HIV, cancer, Alzheimer's, and cardiovascular disease.

We spend $957 billion annually on medical care—more per capita than any other country. No, our health system isn't perfect, but just imagine having appendicitis in Namibia.

VACCINES

During the 1916 New York polio epidemic, the fear was real—even future President Franklin D. Roosevelt got it in 1921. Polio was a devastating disease that would either kill you or leave you unable to walk. It wasn't until 1952 that Jonas Salk first started testing his polio vaccine and determined that it was safe and effective. And not a year too soon. In 1952, the estimated number of cases had reached 57,000. Mass vaccination began immediately, and today polio is all but nonexistent here. Besides polio, we also vaccinate our kids for diphtheria, tetanus, pertussis, measles, mumps, and rubella.

TRANSPLANTS

While the idea of swapping organs goes back to ancient Greek literature, the first successful transplant didn't take place until 1954, and it happened on American soil. When identical twin Richard was dying of kidney disease, brother Ronald offered one of his. Surgeon and researcher Joseph E. Murray performed the first successful kidney transplant at Boston's Peter Bent Brigham Hospital. Americans have also been instrumental in developing successful transplantation methods for hearts, lungs, bone marrow, stem cells, and corneas. Nowadays, it's common practice for Americans to donate organs. In 2000 alone, there were 22,854 organ transplants in our country, giving new meaning to the phrase "have a heart."

THE HUMAN GENOME PROJECT

Funded by the U.S. Department of Energy and the National Institute of Health, the Human Genome Project began in 1990 with a mission to identify and map 30,000 genes in human DNA, as well as to determine the sequences of the three billion chemical base pairs that make up that DNA. The next generation of major medical conquests will arise from this information, especially in the field of cancer. Why? If you can turn off the part of the cell that causes abnormal reproduction (the repressor gene), then you can cure cancers. It's all pretty technical, and we're not really sure what we just said. Just know that the HGP is pretty damn cool, and it's taking place right here in the U.S.A.!

Even More American Medical Milestones . . .

- Accutane
- Acyclovir
- Artificial blood plasma
- Blood banks
- Computerized tomographic scans
- Coronary artery bypass surgery
- Cortisone
- Defibrillator
- Epoetin
- Gentamicin
- Heart valve surgery
- Hepatitis Vaccines
- Imitrex
- Kidney transplants
- Laparoscopy
- MRI
- Nembutal and Pentothal
- Nepogen
- Pancreas transplants
- Pediatric ventilator
- PET scans
- Prozac
- Reanastamosis
- Respirator
- The ultrasound machine
- Vaccination needle
- Xanax

THE PILL

Rubbers suck. You know they suck. They're messy, they reduce sensitivity, and they chafe your privates. But if you're with a partner with a clean bill of health, you don't have to wear 'em, thanks to ten tons of yams and the experimentation of Penn State chem professor Russell Marker.

Marker found that the starchy root contained a hormone-like substance that could inhibit pregnancy. Work and testing continued for the next two decades, and in 1960, America's first affordable oral contraceptive was made available. By 1966, almost 3,000 tons of birth control pills were being taken annually.

Today, 70 million women worldwide are on the pill, and 300 million men are grateful for it.

DID YA KNOW . . . ?

The world's first birth control clinic was opened in Brooklyn in 1916 by maternity nurse Margaret Sanger, who ultimately founded Planned Parenthood.

FUN FACTS

Love, American Style!

We hump more than any other country on earth, with the average American boinking 124 times a year! The Greeks are a close second, while the Japanese get it the least. We also average more partners than anyone else. Let's hear it for variety!

REASON
58

BREAST IMPLANTS

What with our invention of plastic, vulcanized rubber, and Jell-O, it's only natural that we would have come up with breast implants, too.

Around 1960, plastic surgeons Thomas Cronin and Frank Gerow of the Baylor College of Medicine in Texas developed their silicone-gel-filled "mammary prosthesis" with the noble intention of helping women who'd undergone mastectomies. But it wasn't long before chicks from coast to coast seized the opportunity to go from mosquito bites to D cups. Over a million American women had implants by 1990.

Silicone implants caught some flack in the '70s and '80s—something about ruptures and cancer and other nasty stuff—leading many women to opt for inflatable saline-filled ones instead. But after some hefty court settlements, some bankruptcies, and more stringent government regulation, silicone is once again the implant of choice.

In 2000 alone, America racked up an impressive 203,310 breast enhancement procedures—more than double the number in 1997—making us the global leader in this valuable field. Talk about livin' large!

Great American Hooter Havens

SCORES

Watch bouncing boobs in style! Manhattan's "premier gentlemen's club" offers fine dining (they serve a mean lobster), a cigar humidor, and deep tissue massages with its lap dances and pole acrobatics. The antithesis of down-and-dirty neighborhood nudie bars, Scores is all about ass, cash, and flash, catering to a wide range of entertainment stars, athletes, and mobsters. Preferred customers include David Wells, Marky Mark, and Lennox Lewis. By the way, Howard Stern is *always* talking about it, and his hooter standards are pretty high.

THE GOLD CLUB

Hotlanta's Gold Club made many of the popular strip joints in other cities look like PG-rated affairs. It was anything goes, with full nudity, a full bar, and fairly lax rules about where your paws could go during a lap dance. On any given night, you could see A-list celebs like George Clooney, Mick Jagger, Madonna, and Patrick Ewing spilling out of limos or popping bottles of Cristal inside. Even the King of Sweden once dropped in for a private show. Following investigations for alleged mob connections, money laundering, extortion, credit card fraud, police bribery, and prostitution, the club is currently on hiatus. They'll close a joint down for anything these days.

JUMBO'S CLOWN ROOM

Opened in Hollywood in 1970, Jumbo's didn't become an exotic dance club until 1982. Today it's practically a landmark for L.A.'s seedy underbelly. Courtney Love supposedly danced there. David Lynch used to write there. Mick Jagger has been known to pop by. Daryl Hannah did "research" for her film *Dancing at the Blue Iguana* there. It's also the de facto hangout for the authors of this book. Other joints may boast hotter girls and bigger boobs, but Jumbo's is easily the most comfortable, least oppressive strip club in town—probably because it's owned and operated by women. Think of it as the *Cheers* of titty bars. Ask for Karen. Tell her we sent you.

American Racks That Rule...

Loni Anderson
Angeline
Jules Asner
Tyra Banks
Adrienne Barbeau
Erinn Bartlett
Barbi Benton
Halle Berry
Lara Flynn Boyle
Neve Campbell
Cristy Canyon
Catwoman
Natalia Cigliuti
Courteney Cox
Lara Croft
Donna D'Errico
Lolita Davidovich
Bo Derek
Carmen Electra
Elvira
Fat Albert
Farrah Fawcett
Gina Gershon
John Goodman
Camille Grammer
Ginger Grant
Nina Hartley
J-Lo
Janet Jackson
Jenna Jamison
Jewel

American Racks That Rule...

Angelina Jolie

Gypsy Rose Lee

Monica Lewinsky

Lil' Kim

Ms. Lipman
(Dave's 7th-grade teacher)

Heather Locklear

Jayne Mansfield

Rose McGowan

Julie Meadows

Demi Moore

Morgana the Kissing Bandit

Betty Page

Sarah Jessica Parker

Dolly Parton

Tera Patrick

Pandora Peaks

Robin Quivers

Jessica Rabbit

Christina Ricci

Rebecca Romijn-Stamos

Jane Russell

Jeri Ryan

Candy Samples

Jessica Simpson

Tori Spelling

Blaze Starr

Sharon Tay

Tiffani-Amber Thiessen

Uma Thurman

Raquel Welch

Great American Hooter Havens

THE BADA BING

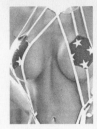

Fans of *The Sopranos* are already familiar with Silvio Dante's strip club, the Bada Bing (A.K.A. The Bing), Tony's and the gang's de facto hangout. Booze, broads, and bullets—how could you go wrong? Unless you get a job on the show, you're pretty much limited to checkin' out the girls on the tube. If you're a lucky slob who lives in the vicinity of Route 17 South in Lodi, New Jersey, you can check out Satin Dolls, the actual club used on the show. *Is the place really run by the mob?* No, but since *The Sopranos* hit the air, mobs of tourists have been comin' in every day to buy *Sopranos* memorabilia and see the hot chicks. Just don't expect to get a blow job in the back room unless you're a "made man."

THEE DOLLHOUSE

For horny teens into heavy metal, their first mental picture of a strip bar comes from Mötley Crüe's classic G-string-infused video for "Girls Girls Girls." Filmed on location in Tampa's legendary Thee DollHouse, the song has gone on to become a stripper anthem that ranks with Kiss's "Lick It Up," Joe Cocker's "You Can Leave Your Hat On," Van Halen's "Hot for Teacher," and Tone Loc's "Wild Thing." *But are those hot girls you saw in the video still working at the club?* Sadly, since the song came out in 1985, most of those dolls have since moved on to become doctors, lawyers, and rocket scientists. On the other hand, you won't be disappointed by the fresh bevy of brazen boobage that now occupies Thee DollHouse's illustrious stage.

SKYBAR

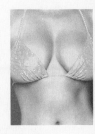

For the most silicone in one place next to Du Pont, try L.A.'s hipster, wannabe-a-celeb hangout, The Skybar, located on Sunset in the Mondrian Hotel, and co-owned by Cindy Crawford's hubby, Rande Gerber. The reservations-only bar features amazing views of the city, the occasional star or model sighting, outrageously priced drinks, attitude up the ass... and a treasure trove of fake racks. Tell girls you're a producer, director, casting agent, or fashion photographer, and you may get to take a pair of those boobs home with you and try 'em for yourself.

ROGAINE

Hair today, gone tomorrow? Well, thanks to Rogaine, there is hope for the follicularly challenged everywhere.

When New Jersey's Upjohn pharmaceutical company developed minoxidil as a blood pressure medicine, physicians noticed an odd side effect on female patients: some grew mustaches! And while the idea of a mustachioed woman might seem quite normal to those with older relatives, the docs studying the phenomenon saw it as a breakthrough. They reasoned: "If it could grow a mustache on a woman, perhaps it could grow hair on a man." Armed with that simple hypothesis, they made a mad dash to figure out just how much minoxidil it would take to help alter the fate of the bald. The result was the topical Rogaine we know today. In regular (2% solution) and extra-strength (5%), it's making a mint for Upjohn.

Merck, another New Jersey-based pharmaceutical company, also took a circuitous route in developing Propecia, a drug initially created to treat enlarged prostates. Patients saw that as their prostrate shrank, their hair grew, and thus sprouted Rogaine's competition.

If you're scared of the rumors that these hair-growing treatments diminish sex drive, there's always Viagra, also available at your local American pharmacy . . . see your doctor.

PAM
ANDERSON

Okay, she's Canadian, but what she stands for is 100 percent American.

In her heyday, the original *Baywatch* babe was a masterpiece of colla-gen and silicone, a testament to the miracles of U.S. cosmetic surgery. If Venus de Milo had arms and lost 20 pounds . . .

Pam and her breasts first got a taste of fame at a football game in her native British Columbia. A roving camera projected her on the arena's Jumbotron screen. When the crowd erupted, Labatt execs signed her up as a spokesmodel. Next came a spread in *Playboy*, followed by the role that made her a masturbatory fantasy for men across the globe: CJ on *Bay-watch*. None of her many subsequent TV and film performances ever matched that powerful opening sequence, where she runs down the beach in slo-mo in a tight red bathing suit, her boobs defying the laws of grav-ity. None, that is, save Pam's home movies with former hubby Tommy Lee, which proved that besides being a hottie, she's also a horn-dog with a very, very deep throat.

Some bitter, ugly chicks call Pam the ultimate icon of bimbosity, but to them we say: *What's wrong with that?* She's parlayed her God-given "talents" into TV production deals and a shitload of money. Let's hear it for the American way!

FUN FACTS

Got Milk?

We sure do! The U.S. is the world's top producer of milk. In 2000, American udders were working overtime to pump out an estimated 84 million tons of the stuff... over twice as much as anyone else!

REASON 61

MUHAMMAD ALI

Few people can rightly claim to be "the greatest of all time." Muhammad Ali is the exception. A fighter in multiple arenas, he'd float like a butterfly, sting like a bee; was as fast with words as he was on his feet; and didn't take shit from The Man. He was a hero to black kids, white kids—hell, almost everyone.

Born Cassius Clay in 1942, he won the Golden Gloves at age seventeen, an Olympic gold medal at eighteen and became heavyweight champ at twenty-two. But this was just the beginning. Converting to Islam and adopting his current moniker, Ali chose jail over going to war, which created one of the largest controversies in sports history and cost him his title. After a brief retirement, he beat George Forman in the "Rumble in the Jungle" in Zaire, and later Joe Frazier in the "Thrilla in Manila." Today he's the only heavyweight champ to hold the title three different times. Out of the ring, he was a great civil rights activist and humanitarian, donating millions to charities, and flying to Iraq to negotiate the release of hostages in 1981.

Most recently, Ali has been honored with a giant Hollywood blockbuster, where he's portrayed by a skinny guy who probably never threw a *real* punch in his life.

THE SUPREME COURT

The U.S. Supreme Court was established as one of three branches of government, with its justices appointed for life. Talk about job security! They don't wear funny wigs, but they do wear robes (clothing underneath optional).

The Court first assembled in New York's Merchants Exchange Building in 1790, under the guidance of Chief Justice John Jay, and since then, folks like Brennan, Holmes, Brandeis, and Marshall have been churning out some of the most eloquent defenses of our civil liberties that you're likely to find.

What makes our Supreme Court so goddamned special? While it can't officially create laws, it has the last say in whether or not a law (or action) is constitutionally on the level. In other words, the buck stops with them. Ours was the first government to vest our judiciary branch with the power to overrule the legislative branch.

From *Marbury v. Madison* to *Roe v. Wade* to the *People v. Larry Flynt*, the Supreme Court has been serving and defining justice for Americans for over 200 years. While not immune to scandal (remember the Coke can and pubic hair?), the Supreme Court justices are the ultimate watchdogs of the Constitution.

Great American Judges

Even More Americans Who "Rule"...

HUGO BLACK

HARRY BLACKMUN

LOUIS BRANDEIS

STEPHEN BREYER

WARREN BURGER

BENJAMIN CARDOZO

SALMON CHASE

WILLIAM DOUGLAS

FELIX FRANKFURTER

ABE FORTAS

RUTH GINSBURG

ARTHUR GOLDBERG

OLIVER HOLMES

CHARLES HUGHES

JUDGE DREDD

JOHN JAY

JUDGE JUDY

JUDGE REINHOLD

JUDGE WAPNER

MIKE JUDGE

DAVE JUSTICE

ANTHONY KENNEDY

JOHN MARSHALL

JAMES MCREYNOLDS

SANDRA O'CONNOR

RUFUS PECKHAM

JOHN MARSHALL

Marshall was the second Chief Justice of the U.S. Supreme Court. Born in 1755, Marshall never received a formal education, but had access to books, and learned to read and write from his parents. Marshall fought in the Revolutionary War, served in Congress and as Secretary of State, and was later appointed to the bench by President Adams (Marshall's close friendship with George Washington helped him land the job). Marshall's majority opinion in the landmark case *Marbury v. Madison* (1803) set the precedent for the Supreme Court to overrule laws made by the President and Congress if the justices deemed them unconstitutional. Marshall is generally credited with turning the U.S. Constitution into a living, breathing, ever-evolving document of law.

THURGOOD MARSHALL

The grandson of a slave, Thurgood Marshall was one of the greatest legal minds ever born in this country. As a practicing lawyer, he won more cases before the Supreme Court than anyone else. Among his victories as counsel for the NAACP were *Sweatt v. Painter* in 1950 and *Brown v. Board of Education* in 1954, which held that racial segregation in schools was unconstitutional. He was first appointed to the U.S. Court of Appeals by JFK in 1961, and LBJ bumped him up to the Supreme Court in 1967, making him the first African-American justice. Here's something you didn't know: Marshall's classmates at Lincoln University included poet Langston Hughes and singer Cab Calloway.

JUDGE MILLS LANE

"Let's get it on!" We love a man with a mantra. You might know him as a judge on his syndicated television show, as a boxing referee in over 100 championship fights, or as the ref in MTV's *Celebrity Death Match*. A former marine, Lane won the NCAA welter-

Great American Judges

weight title in 1960 and barely missed making the Olympic team. Realizing there weren't very many older, short, bald fighters around, Lane went back to school, earned a law degree, and went to work for the district attorney's office in Las Vegas. On the side, he refereed boxing (hey, he lives in Vegas). His most famous decision was to stop the Tyson-Holyfield fight after Tyson ate part of Holyfield's ear.

Even More Americans Who "Rule"...

WILLIAM REHNQUIST

ANTONIN SCALIA

DAVID SOUTER

JOHN STEVENS

POTTER STEWART

HARLAN STONE

WILLIAM HOWARD TAFT

CLARENCE THOMAS

EARL WARREN

BUSHROD WASHINGTON

BYRON WHITE

HERE COMES DA JUDGE...

William Howard Taft is the only person to have served as both the president and supreme court chief justice.

ENTREPRENEURIAL
SPIRIT

Whether you work in a mall or own a Fortune 500 company, congratulations, you're an active participant in American capitalism. Under capitalism, you can start with nothing, and through your own sweat and toil make a fortune. See, self-reliance and self-determination are part of our national psyche. Because America is a young, wide-eyed, bushy-tailed country, it seems like anything is possible here.

Though we're home to some of the biggest businesses in the world— General Electric, General Motors, Microsoft—no one really knows where the next great U.S. company will come from. Banks and venture capitalists are always on the lookout for new talent and new ideas to fund. Some of these ideas come in the form of business proposals, others start at home. Apple computer and Mattel toys? In the garage. Famous Amos Cookies? In the kitchen. Yahoo? In a dorm room. You can come up with your own plan, grow things from the ground up, and you don't need Big Brother's approval to do it. Sure, the government gets a taste in the form of taxes, but they pretty much stay outta your beeswax. It doesn't work that way in communist or socialist countries.

It's not just about coming up with a product that everyone needs, either; it's about creating a need and exploiting the shit out of it any way you can. American history is rife with stories of people who came up with an idea, successfully marketed it, and made bank.

Domino's. UPS. The Pet Rock. Bacon-of-the-Month Club. This book. No dream is too stupid … if it sells.

American Entrepreneurs Who Rule!

BILL GATES

So what if Anthony Michael Hall played him in the movie?! Consider that 99 percent of the world's computers run using his software. That'll give you an indication of his importance. Born in Seattle, Gates and high school pal Paul Allen started Microsoft … and the rest is history. Did he graduate from college? Hell, no! Today, he's so friggin' rich that in 1999 he donated $6 *billion* to charity! Microsoft software accomplishments include MS-DOS, Windows, Word, Excel, Powerpoint, Internet Explorer, and others. Not bad for a skinny geek with glasses.

ANDREW CARNEGIE

Ahh, the classic story of a Scottish immigrant who came to America, worked hard, made good, then saved the U.S. government from bankruptcy during the Great Depression. Oh, did we mention he had this weird condition that caused his nose to more or less melt away? At one point Carnegie controlled more than 25 percent of America's steel production, before cashing out his empire in 1901 for $250 million—roughly $32.5 billion in today's dinero. He spent the rest of his life giving that money away, and to this day, various Carnegie foundations con-

Even More American Entrepreneurs Who Rule…

John Jacob Astor
Ben & Jerry
Arthur Blank
Diamond Jim Brady
Joseph R. Canion
Al Capone
Dick Clark
Michael Dell
Barry Diller
P. Diddy
Walt Disney
T. C. DuPont
Richard Foos
Elmer J. Fudd
George Haley Garrison
David Geffen
Amadeo Peter Giannini
John Gotti
Merv Griffin
Andrew Grove
Ruth Handler
William Hewlett
Colis P. Huntington
Ice-T
Steve Jobs
Magic Johnson
Jeffrey Katzenberg
Will Keith Kellogg
Philip Knight

Even More American Entrepreneurs Who Rule...

Suge Knight

Ray Kroc

Estée Lauder

Ralph Lauren

George Lucas

Bernie Marcus

Master P

Louis B. Mayer

William McGowan

Tom Monaghan

Gordon Moore

J. P. Morgan

Samuel Morse

Pierre Omidyar

David Packard

John D. Rockefeller

Anita Roddick

Colonel Sanders

David Sarnoff

Howard Schultz

Charles Schwab

Bugsy Siegel

Fred Smith

Tony Stark

Martha Stewart

Dave Thomas

Thomas Watson Jr.

Larry Weinbaum

Oprah Winfrey

American Entrepreneurs Who Rule!

tinue to contribute to libraries, schools, and other worthy causes... proof that a free-market spirit doesn't necessarily make you a selfish prick.

RON POPEIL

But wait, there's more! You may not know his name, but you sure know his work. The Chop-O-Matic, Dial-O-Matic, Veg-O-Matic, Mince-O-Matic, Pocket Fisherman, Inside-The-Shell Electric Egg Scrambler, Automatic 5-Minute Pasta and Sausage Maker, and more! Who *doesn't* want this stuff? The founder of Ronco, Ron has made a fortune out of making your life just a little bit easier, especially if you sit around the house and watch TV all day. These days, you can catch Ron making chicken "that used to take an hour" in a mere twenty minutes on infomercials that play more than *I Love Lucy* reruns.

American Businesses That Rule!

WAL-MART

Sam Walton opened his first Wal-Mart store in Arkansas in 1962 with a dream. We're unsure exactly what that dream was, but in 1970 he took the company public, and by 1991 Wal-Mart had become America's largest retailer, with 1,700 stores. In 2001, *Fortune* magazine listed Wal-Mart as its #2 revenue-producing company, just a few million shy of Exxon Mobil. It also made *Fortune*'s lists for "Most Admired Companies" and "Best American Companies to Work For." Needless to say, Exxon didn't make *those* lists. Dig this: every two days, Wal-Mart opens a superstore, and it has a larger computer system than the Pentagon.

FEDEX

You gotta love the FedEx story. As an undergrad at Yale in 1965, Fred Smith wrote a term paper about how most air freight shippers use a bad passenger route system. His paper got a "C," but that didn't stop Fred. In 1971, he started

American Businesses That Rule!

Federal Express with fourteen small planes delivering packages to twenty-five cities. Though he didn't make any dough until 1975, FedEx now delivers 3.3 million packages each busy day, and rakes in a bundle every year. Whose ass hasn't been saved by these guys? They, too, made *Fortune*'s list of best places to work. They're so cool, they allow any of their 143,000 worldwide employees to hitch a ride on their planes for free!

NEWMAN'S OWN

Newman's own started out as a nice little gift actor Paul Newman gave friends one year: a homemade bottle of salad dressing. After numerous requests from his friends for more of his dressing, Paul decided to start selling it, then donate all after-tax profits to charity. So successful was his little side job that the first-year profits amounted to around a million bucks. True to his word, he gave it all away. Since starting the company in 1982, Newman's Own has added pasta sauce, popcorn, lemonade, salsa, and steak sauce to its roster and has donated over $100 million to various charities. Women around the globe are still eagerly awaiting Newman's Own Sockarooni Edible Undies!

BACON-OF-THE-MONTH CLUB

In America there are tons of ways to bring home the bacon: hard work, marry rich, win the lotto, etc. Or you can simply click online and have the bacon delivered to your home! In the glorious tradition of the Harry & David's Fruit-of-the-Month Club and the Book-of-the-Month Club comes the Bacon-of-the-Month Club, brought to you by the industrious folks at GratefulPalate.com. Featured on *The Tonight Show with Jay Leno*, the service offers select artisan handmade bacons from suppliers all over the country, cold-packed and shipped to your doorstep ... ready for sizzling. If fatty cured meat ain't your bag, Grateful Palate can also hook you up with great wines and other assorted goodies, but their big claim to fame is Bacon-of-the-Month. A great gift, it'll make any devout carnivore as happy as a pig in shit.

Even More American Businesses That Rule...

ALBERTSON'S
APPLE COMPUTERS
AT&T
BANK OF AMERICA
BOEING
CHAMPS
CHEVRON
DELL COMPUTER
DISNEY
FORD
THE GAP
GENERAL MOTORS
HEWLETT-PACKARD
HOME DEPOT
IBM
J.P. MORGAN CHASE
LIMITED
L. L. BEAN
LOWE'S
MCDONALD'S
MERRILL LYNCH
MET LIFE
MOTOROLA
OFFICE DEPOT
PARAMOUNT PICTURES
PFIZER
PROCTER & GAMBLE
SAFEWAY
SOUTHWEST AIRLINES
STAPLES
STATE FARM
TARGET
TIME WARNER
TOYS "Я" US
UPS
VERIZON COMMUNICATIONS
WHEREHOUSE MUSIC
XEROX

REASON
64

HUGH HEFNER

He wasn't the first guy to get Marilyn Monroe naked, but he was the first to print the pictures. A capitalist in the truest sense, Hugh Hefner seized an opportunity and gave men what they wanted: photos of hot nude chicks! In the process, he helped usher in the sexual revolution; made bachelorhood acceptable; and introduced the concept of men's fashion.

Hefner, born in 1926, in Chicago was gifted with a genius IQ (as well as an enormous libido). After two years in the army, he earned a degree from the University of Illinois, simultaneously doing cartoons for the *Daily Illinois* and editing the campus humor magazine. After college, he worked in jobs in advertising and publishing before trying to finance his own magazine. Borrowing dough from his mom, and taking out a bank loan using his furniture as collateral, he acquired nude photos of Marilyn and laid out the first issue of *Playboy* on his kitchen table in 1953. It sold 50,000 copies, kicking off the biggest adult entertainment franchise in the world.

★ **148** ★

Today, the magazine has a worldwide circulation of 4.5 million, while Playboy Enterprises Inc.—run by Hugh's daughter, Christie—has net revenues of $350 million a year. Competing mags show more skin, but *Playboy*'s Playmates are still the hottest.

Now in his seventies, Hef remains the ultimate playboy. Cold-kicking it in silk pajamas, throwing wild parties at his infamous Playboy Mansion, and dating three to four bunnies at a time (Viagra, baby!), he's venerated by aspiring men of leisure everywhere.

YOU DON'T READ IT FOR THE ARTICLES, BUT . . .

In its early years, Playboy *nurtured the careers of writers like Lenny Bruce, John Updike, Jack Kerouac, and Alex Haley, printing outspoken views that other magazines wouldn't.*

FAT JUICY
CHRONIC BUDS

They say the grass is always greener on the other side of the fence, but if you're a real patriot, you smoke domestic.

In fact, it's no sacrifice at all to say "no" to foreign bud. Once upon a time, American potheads were dependent on far-off lands like Indonesia, Thailand, Jamaica, and Mexico for their herbal needs, but these days, Indo, Thai Stick, and Mexican "stress" are nothing compared to the potent hybrids grown in Humboldt, or the hydroponic strains found in many a suburban closet. Weed is our fourth-largest cash crop, grossing a cool $15 billion annually.

Of course, it's still contraband in this country—something many folks debate—but as far as quality, rapper D-Dub puts it best: "I wish they all could be California buds."

Now, if we could only be as self-reliant with our oil.

HOT
PIZZA

★ DELIVERED IN 30 MINUTES OR LESS ★

Do you know any other place on earth where you can be high as a kite on your couch with a serious case of the munchies, pick up the phone, and have a hot, bubbling pizza at your door in thirty minutes? Hell, no!

We may not have invented 'za, but we're responsible for Domino's and any number of other methods for instant gratification.

THE DISH
ON PIZZA

In May 2001, Pizza Hut made history
when they delivered pizza to the space station!
Though the personal pan-sized cheese pizza
had to be reheated, the pizza was thoroughly
enjoyed. No word if the delivery guy
got a good tip or not.

FUN FACTS

We're #1!

You'd think that landing on the moon would be enough for the rest of the world to realize how cool we are, right?! Just in case anyone out there has any doubts, here's a list of more #1 U.S. accomplishments:

★ Nobel prizes ★

★ Olympic gold medals ★

★ Largest navy ★

★ Health care spending ★

★ Most marriages ★

★ Largest defense budget ★

★ Largest protected parks ★

★ Longest bridge ★
(Verrazano Narrows, NY)

★ Most university students ★

★ Largest library ★
(Library of Congress)

★ First Manned Lunar Landing ★

★ Book market ★

★ Salt producer ★

★ Greatest coal reserves ★

★ Most VCRs ★

WHITE CASTLE

For the last eighty years, White Castle has been serving their patented "steam-grilled" hamburgers to a hungry nation. Although the chain's name was chosen to signify purity and cleanliness, that hasn't kept fans from giving the square, perforated (so they don't have to be turned over on the grill) sandwiches less savory nicknames such as "sliders," "belly bombs," or "murder burgers." A Midwestern and East Coast phenomenon that's been documented in rhyme by the Beastie Boys, the White Castle experience can now be had across the nation. You can find the burgers in the frozen food section, and they taste just as good fresh from the microwave as they do from the grease-stained "to go" sack.

White Castle claims to sell over 500 million burgers a year, which, given their minuscule size, is about as much as a single Quarter Pounder. But we still love and eat 'em by the bagful whenever the opportunity presents itself!

Even More Fast Food That Rules...

A&W Root Beer

All-American Burger

Arby's

Carl's Jr.

Checkers

Dairy Queen

Del Taco

Der Weinerschnitzel

Dunkin' Donuts

El Pollo Loco

Fatburger

H. Salt Fish & Chips

Hardee's

Jack in the Box

Nathan's

Numero Uno

Pat's King of Steak

Pinks Famous Hot Dogs

Pizza Hut

Popeye's

Poquito Mas

Ray's Famous Pizza

The Salt Lick

Subway

American Fast Food Favorites

MCDONALD'S

What would childhood have been like without Mom taking the family to McDonald's? This is every kid's idea of good eats! Founded in San Bernardino, California, by Dick and Mac McDonald, the golden arches didn't really take off until a milkshake-machine distributor named Ray Kroc convinced the brothers to open more locations, or "franchises." The year was 1954. Kroc opened the first franchise in Des Plains, Iowa, and the rest is history. Ronald McDonald, a 1963 invention, is now the second most recognized character next to Santa Claus, and Mickey D's sells millions of burgers across the globe every year. And the debate ends here: Their fries are, hands down, the best.

KRISPY KREME

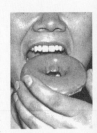

Simply the freshest, best-tasting donut around, made in front of your eyes! When Vernon Rudolph first opened his donut shop in Paducah, Kentucky, in 1933, he had no idea how many people would someday be getting fat on his delicious, deep-fried treat. Within a few years, Vernon relocated his company to Nashville and opened shops in West Virginia and Georgia. Now, with several hundred locations around the nation, almost everyone can enjoy these krispy pillows of sugary goodness, which simply melt in your mouth. We recommend a dozen of the original glazed and a supersized cup of Joe.

KFC

Hey, if you want chicken that's "finger-lickin' good," it's gotta be Colonel Harland Sanders's original-recipe Kentucky Fried Chicken! Born in 1890, Sanders was a cook by trade and never fought in any war, but Kentucky Governor Ruby Laffoon (his real name) loved his chicken so much that he made him a colonel. It wasn't until Harland "retired" that his fame started to sizzle. Deciding that he didn't want to be doomed to a Social Security check and life in a rocking chair, he got back into the chicken biz with his recipe of eleven herbs and spices. He criss-crossed the country by car, hawking his recipe to hungry restaurateurs eager to give him a nickel a chicken for rights to a KFC franchise. By the way, the rumors that KFC uses genetically altered, featherless chickens, and that Colonel Sanders's own remains were battered and deep-fried, are both untrue.

Even More Fast Food That Rules...

The Sunset Grill

Superdog

Taco Bell

Taco Burrito Palace

Tail O' the Pup

Tommy's Burgers

Uno's

Waffle House

Wendy's

FUN FACTS

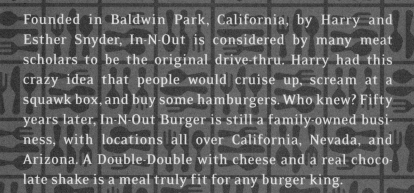

The Ol' In-N-Out!

Founded in Baldwin Park, California, by Harry and Esther Snyder, In-N-Out is considered by many meat scholars to be the original drive-thru. Harry had this crazy idea that people would cruise up, scream at a squawk box, and buy some hamburgers. Who knew? Fifty years later, In-N-Out Burger is still a family-owned business, with locations all over California, Nevada, and Arizona. A Double-Double with cheese and a real chocolate shake is a meal truly fit for any burger king.

REASON
68

WHEELCHAIR ACCESSIBILITY

America is all about inclusion, regardless of race, color, religion, gender, sexual orientation, or disability. Or at least that's the goal.

Now, we're not trying to get all "politically correct" on your ass, but you've got to be damn proud of the fact that our country has been a forerunner in the effort to make life easier and more productive for the disabled. Among other innovations, we built the first folding, tubular steel wheelchair in 1932, and pioneered TV's closed captioning for the hearing-impaired in the early 1970s.

Meanwhile, like the Equal Pay Act, Civil Rights Act, Age Discrimination Act, and Equal Employment Opportunity Act before it, the Americans with Disabilities Act protects the disabled from discrimination in the workplace. We build our buses, trains, and other systems of mass transit with the disabled in mind, and all newly erected buildings and public restrooms must be wheelchair-accessible.

We also created the National Wheelchair Basketball Association (NWBA), the Ms. Wheelchair organization, and the Special

Olympics. We build off-road wheelchair bikes for the disabled thrill-seeker, and there was even a Wheelchair Barbie. True, Mattel was a bit embarrassed when they realized the original Barbie Dream House wasn't wheelchair-accessible, but hell, they still get an "A" for effort, right?!

DISABLED AMERICANS WHO INSPIRE US ...

FDR (President), Stevie Wonder (musician), Ray Charles (musician), Helen Keller (writer/lecturer), Christopher Reeve (activist/director), Bob Dole (senator), Michael J. Fox (actor), Marlee Matlin (Oscar winner), Matt Murdoch (blind daredevil), Muhammad Ali (former boxer/humanitarian), Jim Abbott (pitcher), Chris Burke (actor, *Life Goes On*), Marla Runyan (Olympic runner), Heather Whitestone (Miss America, 1995), Erik Weihenmayer (blind mountain/ice climber), Teddy Pendergrass (musician), James Brady (activist), Ironside (former cop/attorney), Forge (inventor/superhero).

CARTOONS

What do Mickey, Bugs, Daffy, Taz, Snoopy, Calvin, Fred, Huckleberry Hound, the Road Runner, Li'l Abner, Betty Boop, the Katzenjammer Kids, Garfield, Dilbert, Heathcliff, Homer Simpson, Beavis and Butt-Head, Ren & Stimpy, Fat Albert, Lil' Pimp, Opus, Zonker, and Akbar and Jeff all have in common?

They were all born and bred in the U.S. of A.

From the Cold War undertones of *Rocky & Bullwinkle* to the pithy irony of *The Far Side* to the majesty of Disney's *Fantasia*, our cartoons range from brilliant escapist entertainment to politicized commentary— often in the same cell or caption bubble.

As far as we're concerned, our 'toons are tops. And for you skeptics who point to Japanese animé, or Japanimation, did you know that whole trend was inspired by the American-made, feature-length sci-fi 'toon *Heavy Metal* back in the '80s?

American Examples of Fine Tooning!

COMIC BOOKS

Cavemen might have invented art, and Guttenburg the printing press, but it was Ohio's own Richard Felton who is credited with creating the first comic book. In 1863, Felton came up with the "thought bubble," thereby paving the way for the likes of Superman, Spider-Man, Teenage Mutant Ninja Turtles and all the others. With cheap paper plentiful, comic books flourished during the early part of the twentieth century—known as comics' "Golden Age." DC Comics' introduction of slick, square-jawed superheroes like the Flash and the Green Lantern in the '60s ushered in the "Silver Age." When Stan Lee took over Marvel's reins, his more realistically rendered heroes were tragic characters, with problems just like everyone else (Green Arrow's sidekick "Speedy" shot heroin, for instance)—kicking off the "Bronze Age." Today, dark, nihilistic antiheroes like Frank Miller's Batman and Todd McFarland's Spawn are equally concerned with justice and a three-picture deal with Paramount—truly making this the "Show Me the Money Age" of comic books.

R. CRUMB

The iconoclast behind counterculture comix like Fritz the Cat, Mr. Natural, and Devil Girl was born in 1943 in the Philly projects. A fucked-up childhood—Dad was a bully, Mom was strung out—no doubt led to his twisted view of the world. His career in comic illustration began at a greeting card company in Cleveland, Ohio, in the early '60s. He later moved to San Francisco, where he created Mr. Natural ("Keep on truckin'!") and *Zap Comix*, filled with a mix of kinky sex and social commentary. The hippies loved him, even though he made fun of them. Hell, he made fun of everyone. Today he lives in a big château in France. We recommend seeing the documentary *Crumb*. It does his talent and overall bizarreness more justice than we can.

Even More Cartoon Characters That Rule...

Archie

Aquaman

Batman

Yogi Bear

Johnny Bravo

Betty Boop

Bugs Bunny

Captain Marvel

Casper the Friendly Ghost

Charlie Brown

Chip & Dale

Dagwood & Blondie

Daffy Duck

Daredevil

Dexter

Dick Tracy

Donald Duck

Elmer Fudd

The Fantastic Four

Felix the Cat

The Flash

Goofy

The Green Hornet

The Green Lantern

Hawkman

Hulk

The Human Torch

Iron Man

Even More Cartoon Characters That Rule...

Justice League of America

Katzenjammer Kids

Lil' Pimp

Little Lulu

Little Orphan Annie

Magilla Gorilla

Marvin Martian

Mickey Mouse

Mutt and Jeff

The Phantom

Popeye the Sailor

Porky Pig

The Powerpuff Girls

Road Runner

Samurai Jack

Sandman

The Shadow

Silver Surfer

Space Ghost

The Spectre

Spider-Man

The Sub-Mariner

Tweety

Wile E. Coyote

Wonder Woman

X-Men

Yosemite Sam

American Examples of Fine Tooning!

MATT GROENING

Before *The Simpsons* burst on the scene in 1989, there hadn't been an animated series on prime time in over twenty years. And who would have guessed that this crudely drawn show about a fucked-up family would hit such a nerve. Over ten years later, it's the longest-running animated show ever. Matt grew up in Portland, Oregon, in a middle-class family, including his father, Homer, mother, Marge, and sisters, Lisa and Maggie. Sound familiar? Moving to Los Angeles in his piece-of-shit car, he landed a job working for *Los Angeles Reader* magazine, where he was everything from a delivery boy to a rock critic until they offered him a weekly comic strip. His "Life in Hell" strip, featuring fez-wearing duo Jeff and Akbar, proved that you didn't need to be a good artist to be an effective cartoonist. He was later approached to take his dysfunctional brand of 'toons to the small screen, paving the way for *Ren & Stimpy, Beavis & Butt-Head, South Park*, and others.

WE'RE FUNNY!

So this priest walks into a bar... Why did the chicken cross the road? Take my wife, please! Did somebody step on a duck? How many frat boys does it take to screw in a lightbulb? Knock, knock. Pull my finger! And the duck says, "Get this guy out of my ass!"

We're not just funny; we're fucking hilarious! From Ben Franklin's quips in *Poor Richard's Almanac* to the physical comedy of the Keystone Cops to Bill Maher's political satire, America has more humor per capita than any nation on earth. The French? Not funny. The Japanese? Not particularly funny. The Germans? Really not funny at all. Ultimately, what makes our sense of humor so great is that in addition to laughing at others, we're able to laugh at ourselves.

Exactly what makes us crack up? Well, as Ernest Hemingway said: "A man's got to take a lot of punishment to write a really funny book." Translation: Some of America's funniest comedians were those who suffered adversity and injustice, then poked fun at it. Others just poked each other in the eye and acted like morons. Then there's the evening news and reality TV, which don't mean to be funny.

Even More American Comedians Who Rule...

Abbott & Costello

Woody Allen

Jack Benny

Milton Berle

Jack Black

Lenny Bruce

Burns & Allen

Johnny Carson

George Carlin

Rodney Dangerfield

Dr. Demento

Phyllis Diller

Jimmy Durante

Chris Elliott

Jeff Foxworthy

Al Franken

Janeane Garafalo

Bill Hicks

Richard Jeni

The Jerky Boys

Spike Jones

Andy Kaufman

Sam Kinison

Robert Klein

Denis Leary

Richard Lewis

America's Funniest!

RICHARD PRYOR

For our money, the funniest fucking guy to ever stand up next to a microphone. Where do you start? His grandmother owned a brothel, his mom was a prostitute, his father was a pimp, and he grew up in a bad part of Peoria, Illinois (is there a good part?). Television didn't always know how to handle a comic like Pryor, who was entertaining as hell but just too risqué for prime time. Though he made plenty of TV appearances in the late '60s, most of us first got to know Pryor from his naughty—no, filthy—records. After co-writing *Blazing Saddles*, he went on to star in and write movies such as *Silver Streak* and *Stir Crazy*. While setting himself on fire was definitely *not* funny, most contemporary comedians cite him as an influence and hero.

CHRIS ROCK

When Chris Rock is on, he is the funniest comedian and cultural critic on the planet. His outrage is targeted, his material is not sugar-coated with apologies, and his delivery is spot-on. Born and raised in Brooklyn, Rock spent three years on the cast of *Saturday Night Live* and did several forgettable movies. He was fine, it's just that the movies were forgettable. He finally started getting mainstream notice with his HBO specials, followed by his HBO series *The Chris Rock Show,* where he fine-tuned his shtick to a razor-sharp point. Pick up his CD *Bigger and Blacker*—today.

MARGARET CHO

This angry Korean American loves to make fun of Asian stereotypes, sex, gender politics, and herself. Born in San Francisco, Cho started performing standup at sixteen. Moving to L.A., she landed her own sitcom, *All-American Girl*. But when ABC decided she was too chunky and needed an "Asian consultant" to help her be more "Asian," she went on a sex, pills, and booze bender. But what didn't kill her made her stronger. Drawing hilarity from her pain, she has become one of the funniest female comedians in the country, winning several comedy awards, performing Off-Broadway, and appearing in numerous films, including her own live concert movie, *I'm the One That I Want*. Oh, and she used to bang Quentin Tarantino.

America's Funniest!

REDD FOXX

For years we thought our grandfather made up all the dirty jokes he used to tell us, but then we heard a Redd Foxx album and realized that Gramps stole all his material! Born John Sanford in St. Louis, Montana, Foxx picked up the name Redd Foxx while working as a dishwasher with Malcolm X (both had been given the name Red because of their hair color). Foxx's dirty records are legendary and stand the test of time. When he was hired to do a show for NBC, he named his character after his brother, Fred Sanford, who had died a few years earlier.

CHEECH & CHONG

East L.A. native Cheech Marin moved to Canada to dodge the draft (hey, would you want him defending your country?), and met Tommy Chong at Tommy's brother's topless comedy club in Vancouver. The Latino-Asian duo clicked, and hit the road doing standup. Settling in L.A., they were discovered by a record exec who dug their sophomoric jokes about drugs and, well, more drugs. Their lucrative comedy record career led to classic flicks like *Up in Smoke* and *Nice Dreams*. Once the era of "Just Say No" kicked in, Cheech and Chong's popularity waned, and the duo split in '84. Their last appearance together was in 1993's *Far Out Man*, reportedly seen by over eight people nationwide. These days, Cheech keeps busy with tons of TV and film roles, while Chong chills in the bathtub with a fat spliff, waiting for a big C&C reunion movie.

THE MARX BROTHERS

Since Gummo and Zeppo really don't count as real Marx Brothers (they were not very funny), let's just stick to Groucho, Harpo, and Chico. Born in New York of Jewish immigrant parents, The Marx Brothers got their start in vaudeville, but their shtick was so funny, they quickly got movie offers. With the mustachioed Groucho as the lead, and Italian-accented Chico and pantomiming Harpo in support, they produced some seriously funny shit, including *A Day at the Races, Animal Crackers, Duck Soup,* and *Room Service*. Here are a few zingers from Groucho: "I never forget a face, but in your case I'll be glad to make an exception." "I must say that I find television very educational. The minute somebody turns it on, I go to the library and read a book." And, our favorite, "If I held you any closer I would be on the other side of you."

Even More American Comedians Who Rule...

Wendy Liebman

Bernie Mac

Steve Martin

Breasty McFeely

Larry Miller

Martin Mull

Eddie Murphy

Bob Newhart

Penn & Teller

Carl Reiner

Joan Rivers

Paul Rodrigues

Rita Rudner

Adam Sandler

Rob Schneider

Jerry Seinfeld

The Smothers Brothers

Jon Stewart

Keenan Ivory Wayans

Robin Williams

Henny Youngman

SPACE

It's the final frontier, and we conquered it. We weren't the first to make it to the stars (that was the Russkies), but shuttle for shuttle and satellite for satellite, we're the galaxy's Top Dogs. John F. Kennedy started NASA during the Cold War with a pledge that we'd make it to the moon before anyone else—and by golly, we did.

In 1969, Neil Armstrong was the first of twelve men—all Americans— to walk on the moon. Today, ours is still the only flag flapping on that pocked lunar surface, and we continue to lead the earth's exploration of space.

If you believe the tabloids, we also lead the world in UFO sightings and alien abductions.

STAR INVENTIONS . . .

Tang, Velcro, and UV-blocking sunglasses are all American by-products of space travel!

Spacey Achievements!

NEIL ARMSTRONG

When Neil Armstrong hopped out of Apollo 11 and took one small step for man, one giant leap for mankind, planting a flag on the lunar surface, he instilled a sense of national pride in us that remains unmatched. Born in Ohio in 1930, Armstrong received a Bachelor of Science degree in aeronautical engineering from Purdue University and a Master of Science degree from the University of Southern California. Before his big trip to the moon, he was a naval aviator and test pilot. His first space flight was in 1966, when he and fellow astronaut David Scott performed the first successful docking between two vehicles in space.

SPACE SHUTTLE

In 1981, America launched the next chapter in human space travel: the space shuttle orbiter *Columbia*, a reusable winged craft that reached a velocity of 17,322 statute miles per hour, circling the globe in under two hours. After thirty-six orbits, Columbia landed like a normal aircraft at Edwards Air Force Base in California. The promise of this American-built technology is that future generations may have safe, easy access to the stars. Here's a cool shuttle story: In 1962, astronaut John Glenn was the first American to circle the earth. Almost forty years later, U.S. Senator John Glenn returned to space on the shuttle *Discovery*, thus becoming the oldest man in space ever!

STAR TREK

In 1966, Captain Kirk and crew launched one of the biggest entertainment franchises in history. Pitched as "*Wagon Train* in space," *Star Trek* not only featured pioneering special effects, but also plot lines that addressed deep moral, social, and philosophical issues. Plus the alien chicks were sexy and scantily clad. The original series' "five-year mission to boldly go where no man has gone before" lasted only seventy-eight episodes, but *Star Trek* was ultimately discovered by a cult audience of rabid "Trekkies," who made it profitable to launch several spinoff shows and movies. To date, the films alone have generated over $1 billion in worldwide revenues, $5 billion if you count video and other crap. In 1997, show creator Gene Roddenberry's ashes were scattered in space along with those of twenty-three other space pioneers and enthusiasts.

Americans Who've Walked on the Moon...

Neil A. Armstrong
Edwin E. "Buzz" Aldrin
Alan L. Bean
Eugene A. Cernan
Charles Conrad Jr.
Charles M. Duke
James B. Irwin
Edgar D. Mitchel
Harrison H. Schmitt
David R. Scott
Alan B. Shepard
John W. Young

Famous American Who's Moonwalked

Michael Jackson

Famous Americans Who've Claimed to Have Seen UFOs...

Muhammad Ali
Art Bell
Jimmy Carter
Jamie Farr
Glenn Ford
Jackie Gleason
Dick Gregory
Will Smith
Mel Tormé

EVEL KNIEVEL

He's either really brave or really stupid.

Born in Montana, Robert Craig Knievel was a champion skier, pro hockey player, miner, insurance salesman, and elk conservationist before becoming the red-white-and-blue-clad motorcyclist we know and love. Early stunts included riding through fire walls, jumping live rattlesnakes, and soaring across the fountains at Caesar's Palace in Vegas (which put him in a coma for a month). World record-breaking jumps over stacks of cars, buses, and trucks followed. Twenty-five years after the fact, the broadcast of his jump over fourteen Greyhound buses in Ohio still holds ABC's *Wide World of Sports* viewing audience record.

Along with his many successes, there were plenty of fuckups, including his $6 million jump across Idaho's Snake River Canyon. His rocket-powered "Skycycle" cleared the quarter-mile chasm, but winds blew him back into the canyon, nearly killing him. Over the course of his life, he's broken thirty-five bones.

Today, "America's Legendary Daredevil" has a display at the Smithsonian and a river in Arkansas named after him . . . just for being a crazy MF who refused to bow to fear, common sense, and the laws of gravity.

CBGB's

Even by the low standards of rock clubs, CBGB's & OMFUG is a dump. On the skid row corner of Bowery and Bleecker, it's a narrow, neon-lit subway car of a room directly below a flophouse. But from this reeking petri dish of a bar grew punk rock.

The Ramones, Talking Heads, Blondie, and the B-52s were all discovered here, performing on a postage-stamp-sized stage, stepping over the bums, broken bottles, and piles of dog poo left by Jonathon, owner Hilly Kristal's pet, who, like everyone else, knew better than to use CB's legendarily skanky bathrooms.

Oh, and if you're wondering, the name stands for Country, Bluegrass, Blues and Other Music for Uplifting Gourmandizers.

Even More American Clubs That Rule...

40 Watt Club
688
9:30 Club
The Apollo Theater
Bar Sinister
The Blue Note
Bluebird Cafe
Boston Tea Party
Cat's Cradle
The Cave
Club Clearview
Crocodile Cafe
The End of Cole Street
Emo's
The Fillmore
First Avenue
Gazzari's
Great American Music Hall
The Knitting Factory
Liberty Lunch
The Limelight
Lounge Ax
The Love Club
Ludlow Garage
Mabuhay Gardens
Max's Kansas City
Maxwell's
McCabes
The Middle East
Muddclub
Paradise Garage
The Roxy
Scuba's
Stone Pony
Studio 54
Tipitina's
The Village Vanguard
The Viper Room
The Warfield
Whiskey A Go-Go
Xenon

American Clubs That Rule!

THE TROUBADOUR

Most rock clubs have a life span only slightly longer than a mayfly's, but the Troubadour bucked the odds and has been one of the hippest rooms in Los Angeles for four decades. Starting as the home for L.A.'s folk-rock scene in the '60s and '70s, it was also the epicenter of late '80s metal bands such as Guns n' Roses, and in the '90s hosted performances by superstars Radiohead, Jane's Addiction, and Lucinda Williams. The Troub is so hardy, it even managed to survive its days as the salon for hair bands like Ratt and Stryper.

CHECKERBOARD LOUNGE

If you can't get no satisfaction, follow the Rolling Stones to Chicago's Checkerboard Lounge. Mick and Keith loved the place so much they even played there in the 1970s, sharing the stage with Muddy Waters. Why? It sure ain't the décor—torn linoleum on the floor and red lights casting an eerie glow. But the Checkerboard has an impeccable pedigree. Opened by Buddy Guy and Junior Wells, it keeps the soul of Chicago South Side blues alive. Today, legends such as Vance Kelly and Magic Slim keep the joint jumping. And it's the only bar where you can see a pink elephant before you start drinking (it's on the roof of the soul food joint next door).

HOUSE OF BLUES

With eight different venues across the country, House of Blues is the biggest club chain with an urban bent. Modeled after old juke joints, House of Blues showcases all types of music, but is the preeminent corporate champion of jazz, blues, R&B, and hip-hop. Unlike more wussy clubs, HOB has never shied away from controversial genres like hard-core rap. In other words, they *represent*. Add a kickin' sound system and pretty good chow, and you've got a winning combination. In addition, the company has a heart. HOB regularly stages inner-city benefit performances, and sponsors youth education programs designed to increase awareness about African-American contributions to our musical heritage. Ironic that it was all started by a geeky white guy.

DISCO

Those rock pundits who declared that "disco is dead" in the early 1980s couldn't have been more wrong. Once thought to be a fleeting, utterly disposable trend, disco has proven to be one of the most enduring musical idioms in the history of pop. Everyone on the planet with a pulse has, at one time, shaken their groove thang to something by Kool and the Gang, Gloria Gaynor, or KC and the Sunshine Band.

And we created it.

Whether you attribute its birth to Sly and the Family Stone's "Dance to the Music" in 1969, "The Hustle," "Get Down Tonight," and "Jive Talkin'" in 1975, or the opening of *Saturday Night Fever* in 1977, disco is undeniably American, from the twirling ball to the white three-piece suit and platforms. More than just a style of music, it spawned club culture—DJs, fancy lighting, groovy fashions—and countless choreographed dances.

Today, Travolta's "threading the needle" shtick is still the most recognizable dance move in the world. And they say America has no culture!

Even More American Dances...

Big Apple

The Bird

The Bump

Cabbage Patch

Cakewalk

The Charleston

The Clam

The Crip Walk

East Coast Swing

Electric Slide

Fox Trot

The Frug

The Grind

The Jerk

Hand Jive

Hokey-Pokey

The Horizontal Rhumba

Humpty Dance

The Hustle

Limbo

Line dancing

Locomotion

Mashed Potato

The Monkey

Moonwalk

Other Great American Dances!

JITTERBUG/SWING

In the late 1920s, jazzman George "Shorty" Snowden wowed Harlem crowds with his rapid, breakaway solo steps. In honor of Charles Lindbergh's dramatic 1927 "hop" across the Atlantic, Shorty dubbed his dance style the "Lindy Hop." In 1938, Benny Goodman brought jazz to the white mainstream via big band swing, and speeded up the Lindy's fancy footwork, spins, and twirls. His dance, essentially the Lindy on steroids, became known as the jitterbug, or swing dancing, which experienced unparalleled popularity in the U.S. from 1935 to 1960. Why the name? A literal interpretation is that the dancers looked like jittering bugs as they bounced about the dance floor, but some maintain it's an American appropriation of the British expression "to bugger," meaning to get down and nasty.

THE TWIST

Rock 'n' roll's first official dance squashed the traditional notion that dancing had to be done by two partners holding each other. Porky teen Ernest "Chubby Checker" Evans was discovered while singing at a Philly poultry market. In 1960, he covered Hank Ballard and the Midnighters' "The Twist," taking out the original song's sexy R&B flavor, putting a carefree spin on it, and adding his own corkscrew dance moves. The new version shot to the top of the charts and set off a craze from *American Bandstand* to China. Today he owns his own line of beef jerky, but he'll always be remembered for creating the first dance that really let kids cut loose.

BREAK DANCING

Invented in the 1970s in the Bronx, New York, break dancing, like the other elements of hip-hop culture (rapping, deejaying, graffiti art), provided a creative outlet for urban youth with limited resources. Park jams were attended by bell-bottomed, Pro Ked-clad "break boys," or "b-boys," who

Other Great American Dances!

would rock out rhythmically to the DJ's break beats. Influenced by karate flicks, the moves steadily got more acrobatic. In 1983, the movie *Flashdance* gave screen time to pioneering breakers the Rock Steady Crew, and suddenly kids across the country were scouring supermarket bins for cardboard boxes to use as buffers between skin and asphalt. Break dancing is currently enjoying a resurgence, with kids flipping on their bellies like fish out of water and spinning on their heads at dance clubs and hip-hop shows across the globe.

Even More American Dances . . .

The Monster Mash

The Mummy

Pogo

Pop-Locking

The Robot

Running Man

The Shag

The Shimmy

Square Dancing

The Swim

Texas Two-Step

Watusi

Walk Like an Egyptian

The White Man's Overbite

The Worm

Vogue

THE LETTER "A"

This page is brought to you by the letter "A."

For many American Gen-Xers, public TV show *Sesame Street* was their first introduction to the alphabet and numbers. "Edutainment" at its best, Kermit, Bert and Ernie, Big Bird, Oscar, and the Cookie Monster made us giggle as we learned about the three R's.

The man behind those loveable puppets was the late Jim Henson. As a freshman at the University of Maryland, he created the daily five-minute show *Sam and Friends* on a local NBC affiliate, featuring future Muppet stars like Kermit. The show was a smash and paved the way for Jim and his growing Jim Henson Company to create *Sesame Street* in '69, and *The Muppet Show* in the mid-'70s. He also founded the Jim Henson Creature Shop, specializing in animatronic visual effects as seen in movies like *Babe* and *The Empire Strikes Back*.

For his neverending imagination, humor, and technical genius, Jim & Co. received a ton of accolades and awards, as well as a warm spot in the hearts of kids and parents nationwide.

The American A-List!

AA

Getting shitfaced is just fine with us ... unless it's all you ever do. Fortunately, for those drinkers who don't know when to say "when," there's Alcoholics Anonymous. AA was started in 1935 in Akron, Ohio, by a recovering alcoholic stockbroker and a hopelessly drunk surgeon. Together, they diagnosed the problem as a disease, not a moral failing, and formed several alcoholics' discussion groups. The groups multiplied, and today, 2,000,000 alcoholics world-wide owe their sobriety to AA and its twelve-step program. The coolest thing about AA is that it works. The second coolest thing is that it's free. Plus, there are no rules; you can even show up bombed. AA meetings are also a great place to see rock stars, sell a screenplay, and hook up!

AAA

When it's dark and pouring rain and your car won't start, who's got your back? These guys. In 1902, a number of locally based auto clubs, comprised mainly of affluent car hobbyists, unified under a single federation called the Automobile Association of America. Back then, AAA's primary mission was to act as the sanctioning body for racing and speed records. Over the years, it evolved into a not-for-profit federation of eighty-six clubs, with more than 1,000 offices serving 43 million members. They'll change your tire, juice your battery, or break in when you've locked your keys inside ... and they won't even give you shit about it.

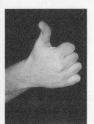

"AAAAYYYYY!"

Back in the '70s, Arthur Herbert Fonzarelli, a.k.a. The Fonz, coupled this catchphrase with a thumbs-up gesture as a sign of approbation or good fortune. An orphan and high school dropout, the Fonz rode with the notorious Falcons motorcycle gang. As he grew older, though, he left gang life to become an auto mechanic. He spent his free time at Arnold's Drive-In, picking up babes and dispensing invaluable wisdom in his "office" to his nerdy pet project, Richie Cunningham. Refusing to let his underprivileged upbringing keep him down, he later attended night classes and got his high school diploma. Even after the Fonz became a respected high school shop teacher, "Aaaayyyy!" remained his trademark phrase.

Even More Great "A's" ...

The A-Team
Abigail Adams
Academy Awards
Ace Frehley
Ace Ventura
Ace Hardware
ACLU
Action-packed!
ADA
The Advocate
Adam 12
Adam Horowitz
Aerosmith
AFL-CIO
Alabama
Alan Alda
Alaska
Ambrosia
AMA
America
AOL
Ansel Adams
Arizona
Arkansas
Arnold's Drive-In
Arby's
Associated Press
Astronauts
Atlanta
Atlantic City
Atom Ant
Austin
Hank Aaron
NAACP
The Oakland A's
T & A

WALL STREET

Like the supermarket, Wall Street offers anything and everything to anyone who wants in. As long as your money's green, you have the opportunity to make more of it, or lose it all.

Built along the route of a wooden stockade made by the Dutch to keep the British and Indians out, Wall Street's beginnings in 1792 as a center of capitalism were modest. Twenty-four brokers met underneath a buttonwood tree at 68 Wall Street and agreed to charge their customers a uniform commission.

Today, 1,366 companies trade on the giant New York Stock Exchange, which employs over 100,000 people. Even though the exchange is technically not on Wall Street (it's located three blocks south, at 20 Broad), the narrow, twisty thoroughfare is still the heart of NY's financial district, with many brokers and investment companies keeping offices there.

Even more than Pamplona, Spain, Wall Street celebrates the running of the bulls. When the market is up, the streets downtown are thick with free-spending brokers in expensive suits, lighting up Cuban cigars; when times are *really* good, they're lit up on Colombian cocaine.

FUN FACTS

We're #2!

2nd country to put a woman in space!

2nd largest number of chickens!

2nd largest producer of timber!

2nd most Nobel Prizes in literature!

2nd largest number of universities!

2nd biggest opera theatre (in St. Louis)!

2nd highest number of movies produced yearly (no shit, India beats us)!

2nd biggest producers of gold and silver!

2nd biggest oil producer!

2nd largest potato chip consumer!

Home to 2nd most deadly lizard on the planet (the gila monster)!

MO' MONEY

There's a reason why *we* coined the phrase, "Show me the money."

We're arguably the richest country on earth. Our yearly expenditure of moola per capita ranks third, but #1 and #2 are a helluva lot smaller than we are. We have the most billionaires (55), and the youngest billionaire (Jerry Yang of Yahoo!). The world's richest living person is our very own Bill Gates ($60 billion), and the richest man of all time is John D. Rockefeller (the $900 million he amassed in 1913 equates to $65.9 billion today). We've also got Paul Allen, Michael Dell, Warren Buffett, Gordon Moore, Eddie Money, and Richie Rich.

Why do we have so much goddamned dough? Well . . . we work for it! America is not an old country rife with aristocratic descendents and centuries-old fortunes. There's certainly some old money floating around, but many of our millionaires and billionaires didn't inherit their wealth; they earned it.

Who wants to be a millionaire? Well, you don't have to be Regis to figure that one out. We all do, and you can get there any way you want: as a lawyer, doctor, inventor, builder, movie star, businessman, novelist, or athlete. Or you can just marry rich.

FIREFIGHTERS

They save kittens from trees and babies from burning buildings, while their big hoses command the attention of women everywhere. Whereas common logic dictates that you run from smoke and flames, these guys walk into it without hesitation.

It's hard to trace which country had the first real fire department, but in America, organized fire fighting began in New York in 1648. Fines for dirty chimneys generated the dough for the maintenance of leather buckets, hooks, and ladders. There were eight fire wardens to stand on fire watch, and every male citizen had to take a turn as warden. In 1731, British hand-drawn pumpers were the first fire engines to be used in the colony.

Today, our firefighters are arguably the best in the world. They handle everything from brush fires to flaming chemical plants to burning oil rigs in other countries. They're tough, they're brave, and they know their shit. There's a reason why, at one time, every American boy dreams of swizzling down that pole, hitting the siren, and rolling out of the station in that big-ass red truck.

CESAR CHAVEZ

He was an advocate for the little man and a voice for the voiceless...
literally. He didn't do it for money or fame, but to help out his peeps
in the fields. As far as we're concerned, he ranks right up there with
MLK Jr.

Cesar Chavez rose from dirt-poor beginnings as an Arizona migrant
farm worker. As a teen, he labored in the fields to help support his family, settling down in San Jose, California, after a stint in World War II.
Knowing firsthand about the appalling job conditions for Mexican-
American farm laborers, he refused to sit by idly. He made speeches
about their rights, led voter registration drives, and ultimately founded
the first successful U.S. farm workers' union (the National Farm Workers Association, later changed to United Farm Workers).

In the mid-'60s, he led a nonviolent strike of California grape pick-
ers to demand higher wages, and encouraged a nationwide boycott of
table grapes. He organized a similar strike for lettuce growers in the
early '70s, and protested against the hazards of toxic pesticides in
the '80s. His efforts ultimately resulted in higher pay, improved

health and pension benefits, and regulations against dangerous pesticide spraying.

A cultural hero to Mexican Americans and Americans in general, Chavez died in 1993 at age 66, and was posthumously awarded the Presidential Medal of Freedom. He was truly the cream of the crop.

FUN FACTS

¡Mi Casa Es Su Casa!

That's right, our great melting pot has a veritable shitload of ingredients. If you have any doubts, here's the proof.

★ **We Speak Your Language!** There are over 329 different languages spoken in the United States, with twenty-seven of them spoken at home by at least 100,000 people.

★ **America's International Buffet!** No matter what country you're from, your native cuisine is readily available at sushi bars, Ethiopian restaurants, kosher delis, burrito joints, ristorantes, and eateries specializing in everything from goulash to fish and chips to chicken vindaloo. Nowadays, your local mall's food court is a veritable smorgasbord of fine international fare.

★ **Choose Your Poison!** Whether you have a taste for Greek ouzo, Russian vodka, fine French champagne, Japanese sake, Foster's, Moosehead, or Tecate, you'll find your favorite imported hooch at most local grocery stores.

★ **Our City Is Your City!** Most major U.S. cities have their own ethnic enclaves. Look for these mini-nations around the country: Chinatown (San Francisco and other cities), Little Italy (New York), Little Havana (Miami), Ukrainian Village and Little Saigon (Chicago), Olivera Street and Thai Town (Los Angeles), and the Adams-Morgan Ethiopian district (Washington, DC).

FUN FACTS

Aliens Dig Us!

We're home to legal and illegal aliens alike. We also have the most alien visitors from outer space. Since a legendary *alleged* UFO crash back in 1947, Roswell, New Mexico, has been considered the "UFO Capital of the World." Every year, thousands of tourists flock to Roswell to catch a glimpse of a flying saucer or other unidentified flying object. And even if they don't, their pilgrimage won't be completely in vain: The city boasts extraterrestrial fun like the International UFO Museum and Research Center. But you don't have to travel to New Mexico to get your fix of E.T. Every year, hundreds of UFO sightings are reported in every state in the union, including Alaska and Hawaii. From the evidence amassed, it seems quite clear that in addition to being the world's most popular vacation spot, we're also the preferred travel destination for life forms throughout the universe.

SHIT
WORKS

Light switches. Phones. Faucets. Traffic lights. A fridge full of cold ones. One of the best things about our beloved country is that shit like this usually works.

When your cable goes out in the middle of a rainstorm or your air conditioning goes out in summer, it feels like the end of the world, right?! Meanwhile, the loss of electricity and other common comforts we take for granted is par for the course in many other countries.

We don't have to worry about a lot of the daily annoyances experienced around the world, which gives us more time to invent stuff, make money, go shopping, watch TV and do nothing.

DID YA KNOW...?

*The United States has more free "working"
public restrooms and drinking fountains than anywhere
else in the world. Just keep an eye out for
Brits like George Michael!*

Even More Shit That Works...

Air-conditioning
Airports
ATMs
Buses
Cable TV
Condoms
Copy machines
Dead animal cleanup
Drains
Drinking fountains
Electrical plugs
Elevators
Emergency Broadcast System
Emergency services
Escalators
Garbage pickup
Gas pumps
Good pickup lines
Hospitals
Hot water
Ice machines
Internet access
Jacuzzis
Mail
Operators
Our government (sometimes)
People
Refrigerators
Roads
Sewers
Trains
Vending machines
Vibrating beds

Shit That Works

TOILETS

Generally speaking, you can usually count on three things with an American toilet: 1) it'll be there, 2) it will probably flush, and 3) things won't come back to haunt you. In America, the idea of having access to your own personal potty is a right, not a privilege. Go to some far-off land and you might be squatting over a hole and using water from a bucket to flush. Ever go to an American hotel without a crapper? Didn't think so. And by the way, it's a *bidet*, not a fountain, bucko. We'll leave that fancy shit for the French. Give us good old American TP any day!

TRAFFIC LIGHTS

You think driving sucks in America? Try driving in other crowded countries in the world where roads are hundreds of years old and were built for horses and buggies. That's one of the advantages of being a young nation. Regulating our roads is an intricate system of traffic lights, which also generally works. Invented by police officer William Potts of Detroit, the first traffic light was a retooled railroad signal. A few years later, Cleveland inventor Garrett Morgan perfected the electric automated traffic light. Who invented those new ticket-making traffic lights that are sprouting all over the country? Well, if you find out, kick their ass for us!

TELEPHONES

Don't take that dial tone for granted! Unless you haven't paid your bill, phones in the U.S. tend to be reliable, and are available to anyone, anytime, day or night; no lines, no waiting, no hassles. Need to call the UK? No operator needed, simply pick up the receiver and dial away. Heck, you don't even need to yell. Now, we're not saying that the phone system is perfect—being stuck on hold waiting for Sprint to fix an error on your bill is like root canal. But you just try having that same sort of conversation when you're out of the country. It's a whole different breed of torture!

EDUCATION

Like your folks once said, "Kid, without an education, you're nobody."

In America, everybody has a right to be somebody, and that means at least twelve years of reading, writing, and arithmetic. The best thing is, it's free! As long as you live here, you can expect to pay nothing for your education right through high school.

Got your pencils ready? Here are some impressive educational stats worth scribbling down: every year in public schools alone, 2.9 million full-time teachers, 620,000 instructional aides, and 96,000 guidence counselors teach 47 million students in kindergarten through twelfth grade. The whole shebang costs taxpayers roughly $334 billion and change. It doesn't take a math whiz to figure out that we place a high importance on elementary and secondary education.

We're no slouches when it comes to higher learning, either. Our 6,000-school university system teaches a world-record 14.2 million students annually! Every year, over 400,000 students from around the globe relocate to the United States just to study at renowned colleges and universities like Princeton, Yale, M.I.T., Stanford, and Berkeley. While British schools like Oxford used to be the standard of excellence, Harvard is now considered by many to be the best university in the world.

FUN FACTS

Fun Classes

Taught in America...

"Basket Weaving"
(University of Pittsburgh at Bradford)

"Queer/Race Studies: Intersections And Genealogies"
(University of California, Santa Cruz)

"Feminist Epistemologies and Pedagogy"
(University of California, Santa Barbara)

"The Simpsons and Philosophy: The D'oh of Homer"
(Siena Heights University, MI)

"Pornography: Writing of Prostitutes"
(Wesleyan University, CT)

**"Understanding the King: The Life
and Music of Elvis Presley"**
(Cal State Fullerton)

"Physics for Poets"
(most universities across America)

"Basics of McDonald's Operations"
(McDonald's Hamburger University, Oak Brook, IL)

"Women's Studies: Female Rappers and Their Messages"
(University of Minnesota)

"Beginning Contortion," "Beginning Aerial Trapeze"
(San Francisco's School of Circus Arts)

"Balloon Sculpture"
(Clown College, MA)

"The Oral Tradition"
(Institute of Fellatio Arts & Sciences)

AMERICAN SLANG

Over the past two centuries, we've turned the King's English into one badass muthafuckin' dialect.

Our language may not be as elegant as French or Italian, or as old as Greek, but American slanguage is off the hizzle fo' shizzle, my nizzle! Folks around the world are familiar with our idiomatic expressions, even when they don't really know what they mean. Without American slang, there'd be no "cool" or "okay," two of the most spoken words on the planet.

Yes, from "asskisser" to "zoning out," ours is a rich lexicon as full of nuance and subtlety as any Romance language. Just think about the verbal resources we have at our fingertips to describe, say, vomiting (barf, blow chunks, toss cookies, Technicolor yawn, hurl) or the engagement in sexual relations (pork, boff, boink, hump, digging out the nappy dugout).

Without our own homespun slang, there'd be no choking the chicken, carpet-munching, ball-bustin', or shot-callin' big ballin'. You wouldn't be able to wig out, give a wedgie, wet your whistle, or take a whizz, and you couldn't dis Five-O, the po-po, or the fuzz. Plus, you'd have no way to refer to preppies, yuppies, buppies, groupies, wiggers, nerds, or dweebs . . . and that would just be bogus.

AMSCRAY

(ĂM-skrā) *Verb intransitive.* A Pig Latin variation of the verb *to scram*, meaning to leave the premises in great haste; get the hell outta Dodge; blow this Popsicle stand.

BENJIS

(BĔN-jēz) *Noun.* Short for Benjamins, as in money, dinero, dough, cash, as in: "It's all about the Benjamins, baby!" *Origin:* "Ben Franklins" originally referred to $100 bills, which are emblazoned with his mug. The term came to mean moola in general.

BI-YATCH!

(BĒ yŏch) Also spelled *biiiii-yatch! Noun* 1) Bitch, as in a trick-ass ho who's only after your Benjamins. 2) A whiny guy or pussy who just sorta rubs you the wrong way, as in: "Gimme those cookies, you biiii-yatch!" *Synonyms:* beeznatch.

BUST YOUR BALLS

(BŬST yuur BAWLZ) *Verb.* To verbally emasculate, to harass or insult in order to break one's spirit, as in: "Just because he burned the baked ziti is no reason to bust his balls." *Origin:* To castrate a calf, the testicles are sometimes broken instead of cut off. Busting balls is the metaphorical equivalent of turning a bull into a steer, a man into a eunuch, thereby robbing him of power and potency. The expression is currently experiencing a spike in popularity due to frequent use by the Soprano family.

CHRONIC

(KRŎNĭk) *Noun.* 1) Potent strain of Cali weed. *Abbreviation:* the chron. 2) Generic reference to weed. *Synonyms:* Indo, sticky-icky, smoke, herb, ganjah, Mary Jane, grass, pot, reefer. *Origin:* Popularized by Dr. Dre and his landmark rap album, *The Chronic.*

COOL

(kool) *Adjective.* 1) Unemotional, reserved, as in: "Keep cool" or "He's cool as a cucumber." 2) Hip, with it, in tune with current trends and fads, in the mix, down wit' dat shit. 3) Expression of approval, as in right on, rockin', that's an excellent turn of events. *Origin:* 1940s jazz scene, or something like that.

COOTIES

(KOOTēz) *Noun (plural).* An invisible body louse contracted by small children when touched by a member of the opposite sex. Highly contagious, cooties are commonly passed about on elementary school playgrounds.

DOH!

(dō) *Interjection.* Oh, shit, dammit, fuck, or any other exclamation when one is generally frustrated or pissed off. *Origin:* Popularized by Homer Simpson of Springfield, U.S.A., it was recently canonized by inclusion in *Webster's Dictionary.*

EAT CROW

(ēt krō) *Verb.* To be proven wrong, eat humble pie, as in: "You told me that having sex with that psycho bitch was a bad idea, and now I'm eating crow." *Origin:* An article published in the *Atlanta Constitution* in 1888 claims that toward the end of the War of 1812, an American went hunting and by accident crossed into British turf, where he shot a bird. He was caught by a British officer, who complimented him on his fine shooting and persuaded him to hand over his gun. The officer then pointed his gun at the American and said that as punishment, he had to take a bite of the bird, feathers and all. The American obeyed, but when the British officer returned his gun to him, the American took revenge by making him eat the rest of the bird.

GAG ME WITH A SPOON

(GĂg mē with a SPŌŌN) *Declaration.* Disgusting, repulsive, grotey, grotey to the max, as in: "Did you see that haircut? As if! Like, gag me with a spoon." Frequently used with the preposition "like" and the interjection "omigod!" *Origin:* The San Fernando Valley, 1980s.

KISSASS

(KĬSǎs) *Noun.* 1) Fawner, sycophant, yes man, butt-smoocher, brown-nose, as in: "His tongue is so far up his boss's ass he can taste his kidneys, he's a real kissass." 2) Suck ass.

OK

(ōKĀ) Also spelled okay. *Adjective.* 1) Acceptable, fine, as in: "I was hammered out of my head last night, but, surprisingly, this morning I'm okay." 2) Passable, mediocre, as in: "He's just okay in the sack." *Origins:* Myth has it that the word comes from the use of initials of Old Kinderhook, the birthplace of U.S. President Martin Van Buren. More likely, the word is derived from the Native American word "okehi," which translates as "may it be so."

WHAT'S THE DIZZLE, MY NIZZLE?

(wŏz da DĬZ el, mĭ NĬZ el) *Idiomatic expression.* 1) What the dilly, yo? 2) What up, my brother? 3) What is going on, my fine brethren? Possible response to aforementioned question: "It's off the hizzle fo' shizzle, my nizzle" ("Things are great!") *Origin:* This hip-hop version of Pig Latin was first introduced via the hizzle shizzle nizzle 80s old-school rap classic "Double Dutch Bus." Snoop Dogg covered the song, reintroducing the long-dormant style of wordplay into the contemporary urban consciousness. Rapper Jay-Z then adopted it and bumped that shiznit to the next level, creating an entire hip-hop lexicon that's harder to decipher than a German U-Boat code. Word up.

ZOINKS!

(zoynkz) *Interjection.* 1) Expression of disbelief or disappointment, as in: "Zoinks! He ate all the Scooby snacks." *Synonyms:* Jeepers, zounds, omigosh, my goodness. *Origin:* Conceived by a goatee-wearing hippie and his talking Great Dane, who together had a proclivity for exposing fake ghosts and ghouls.

MADONNA

She's sold 100 million albums . . . held Dave Letterman captive on his own show . . . was condemned by the Pope . . . and humped some of the biggest names in entertainment. We love Madonna because she's outrageous, talented, and horny.

She's also self-made.

Ms. Ciccone started off as a dancer and backup singer for disco star Patrick ("Born to Be Alive"). She convinced the DJ at New York club Danceteria to play her demos, which led to a deal with Sire Records. Since then, she's continuously pushed the envelope, her songs and videos broaching everything from interracial love to unwed pregnant moms to Jesus's skin color to big dicks (see Tarantino's opening diatribe in *Reservoir Dogs*). Stuffy feminists have criticized her brash "I'm-a-boy-toy-and-proud-of-it" 'tude, but Lady Madonna has proven to be more than just a sexed-up diva. She's a staunch gay rights and AIDS activist, and a formidable businesswoman, starting her own Maverick label in 1992.

Even after squeezing out a couple of pups and hitting her mid-forties, she consistently adapts to current trends and remains a vital force in pop. While some of her aging peers do the same old tired song and dance, Madonna has an uncanny ability to reinvent herself.

FUN FACTS

Madonna Mates

If Ms. Ciccone's lovers were laid end to end, (insert own punch line here). Here are a few of her more famous alleged conquests.

WARREN BEATTY

GUY RITCHIE

JELLYBEAN BENITEZ

BASQUIAT

SEAN PENN

SANDRA BERNHARD

VANILLA ICE

JFK JR.

DENNIS RODMAN

EVIAN BOTTLE*

*As seen in *Truth or Dare.* No confirmation as to whether the bottle enjoyed it.

FREEDOM TO TALK SHIT

Free speech is one of your inalienable rights. Our Constitution guarantees YOU the right to talk any kind of shit you want—even stuff no one else agrees with. Some of our greatest leaders kicked off their careers proposing things that no one wanted to hear: that slavery and later segregation had to go, that women should have the right to vote, that magazine publishers should be allowed to show close-ups of hard-core penetration.

The best part is, the rule applies to all of us, from Martin Luther King Jr. to Larry Flynt to L. Ron Hubbard. Everyone, from the heroic to the asinine, gets a chance to stand on the soapbox. Opinions are like assholes—everyone's got one—and we've got plenty. That's one of the reasons we're cool.

Without the right to talk shit, the *Washington Post* could have never exposed Tricky Dick, comics like Lenny Bruce couldn't have criticized the government, Abbie Hoffman couldn't have demonstrated against the Vietnam War, and NWA couldn't have flipped the bird to the LAPD.

The cornerstone of our democracy, freedom of speech safeguards an open marketplace of ideas, and freedom in general. And if you don't like it, you can use your inalienable right to simply shut the fuck up.

Great American Shit-Talkers!

FREDERICK DOUGLASS

Born in Maryland in 1818, Frederick Douglass escaped slavery, kicked it with abolitionists and social reformers, and served as a stationmaster on the Underground Railroad. Man, was he unpopular Down South! His friendship with Lincoln pushed the Prez to make Emancipation a cause of the Civil War, and Fred helped recruit black troops for the Union Army. But of all his accomplishments, we remember him best for his badass, supereloquent speeches about the brutality and immorality of slavery. He also published *The North Star* and *Frederick Douglass's Paper*, which brought news of the anti-slavery movement to thousands. To be a black man of his time making waves like he did, you know the dude had to have cajones of steel.

WOODWARD AND BERNSTEIN

While most newspapers dismissed a 1972 break-in at Democratic Party headquarters as "a caper," *Washington Post* reporters Bob Woodward and Carl Bernstein smelled a rat. Thanks to perseverance and a few handy tips from Deep Throat, they linked the burglars to Nixon's Committee to Re-Elect the President (CREEP), and the shit hit the fan. Two years later, Nixon resigned. The Watergate scandal may be a blemish in our national history, but the fact that two journalists could take on The Man and bring him down says something great about America. The duo won the Pulitzer Prize, and went on to write a buttload of best-selling books, including *All the President's Men*. If you haven't read it, at least see the movie.

LARRY FLYNT

You think he's a pig who exploits women? Then don't buy *Hustler*! That's your right. But you've gotta support HIS right to print that filth. You've also got to applaud his First Amendment activism. The former strip club owner has fought a number of court battles to safeguard your right to see naked chicks in compromising positions. But his free speech activism goes deeper than that. In 1988, the Supreme Court overruled a $200,000 award to Jerry Falwell for a *Hustler* parody about the preacher getting down with his mom, thereby protecting parody as political satire. Moreover, Larry has publicly aired the dirty laundry of several hypocritical politicians, including the fact that a *certain* President got a gal pregnant, and paid for an abortion while working for Daddy's campaign.

Even More Great American Shit-Talkers...

BOB & TOM

DANNY BONADUCE

WILLIE BROWN

LENNY BRUCE

LUKE CAMPBELL

MARK CUBAN

LARRY ELDER

KEVIN & BEAN

LARRY KING

BOBBY KNIGHT

TOM LYKIS

TRACY MCGRADY

DENNIS MILLER

RALPH NADER

BILL O'REILLY

DENNIS RODMAN

JIM ROME

ANDY ROONEY

PETER TILDEN

BOB UECKER

Freedom of the Press!

These American Rags Generally Say Whatever the Hell They Please!

American Spectator magazine
Atlantic Monthly
Caffeine magazine
Consumer Reports
Cosmopolitan
The Economist
Entertainment Weekly
Forbes
Fortune
Guns & Ammo
High Times
Hustler
Kronick magazine
L.A. Weekly
Mad magazine
Maxim
Men's Health
Mother Jones

The Nation
The National Enquirer
National Geographic
National Lampoon
The New Republic
New Times
The New York Post
The New York Times
The New Yorker
Newsweek
People
Playboy
Rolling Stone
San Jose Mercury News
Science
Source Magazine of Hip Hop
The Star
Stuff
Time magazine
U.S. News & World Report
UTNE Reader
The Village Voice
Vogue
The Wall Street Journal
The Washington Post
Wired

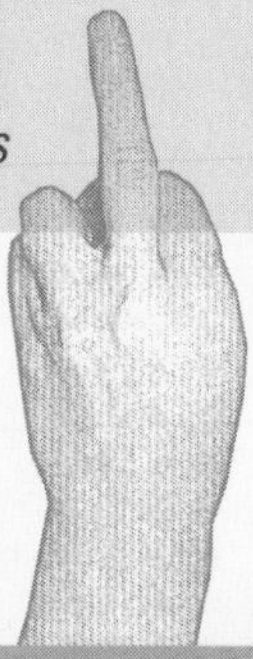

FUN FACTS

The World Record

FOR MOST SHIT TALKED...

The movie *South Park: Bigger, Longer & Uncut* holds the *Guinness Book of World Records* record for most swearing in an animated flick: 399 expletives and 128 obscene gestures.

HOWARD STERN

With insightful political and social satire, Howard Stern kicked the dust off of radio and sent fast-talkin' DJs to their graves. Where would we be without our daily dose of flatulence, boob, and penis jokes? Hell, he should be up for the Nobel Peace Prize for his interviews of Ozzy Osbourne alone!

While many simply dismiss him as a foul-mouthed perv, loyal listeners recognize that he slices and dices through the public relations spin doctors and daily bullshit, and tells it like it is ... while still making us laugh. We're also amazed at his ability to make us salivate when one of his hot stripper guests takes off her clothes ... on the radio! He gets guys to sport wood by sheer power of description, no visuals necessary.

The "King of All Media," Howard has an unprecedented power to reach millions of people through the airwaves, books, and films. His on-air farts are truly the trumpets of free speech, and we love his shtick. Now, if we could only win Fred's money ...

REASON

86

THE ONION

We could have said *USA Today*, but let's face it—it's not funny on purpose.

The Onion embodies the spirit of satire and parody protected by our free speech rights. Every week, this mock newspaper breaks down the silliness of a society fixated on hype and triviality, using ridiculous (and controversial) headlines to hint at hard-hitting realities about the state of the nation and the world.

The paper was started up in 1988 in Madison, Wisconsin, by some weird, unstable, but really funny college students. Recently moving to NYC, *The Onion* has exploded: they've put out a number of best-selling books and calendars, and their website, TheOnion.com, receives 800,000 visitors a month.

Some of our favorite articles include: "Congress Passes 'America Is #1' Bill: 'Whooooo!' Shout Legislators," "Nation's Educators Alarmed by Poorly Written Teen Suicide Notes," "Auto Industry Agrees to Install Brakes in SUVs," and "Area Stoner Regales Other Stoners with Tale of Amazing Super Bong He Saw in Iowa City Once." We also love the brilliant point/counterpoint column, "You the Man/No You the Man." Funny shit.

THE ACLU

Fight the power!

Love 'em or hate 'em, just be happy they're there for you. When our government loses sight of the big picture and oversteps its bounds, who you gonna call? These guys. They've fought on the side of white supremacists as well as Larry Flynt. Their goal is simple: protect the constitution, popularity be damned. What makes America great is that we don't have to like what you say to fight for your right to say it. The American Civil Liberties Union never loses sight of the fact that you have to protect the rights of everyone . . . not just those you agree with.

FOIA

Voted into law in 1967, the Freedom of Information Act requires that government agencies must publish a list of all the files they have, and then allows any citizen to gain access to the info, as long as it's not considered "top secret." There are files on everything from Elvis Presley to Bozo the Clown.

THE NRA

Like the ACLU, the National Rifle Association exists to protect your rights. Specifically, they protect your constitutional right to *pack heat*. Love 'em or hate 'em, be happy they're there, because as soon as you start chipping away at the Constitution, the bedrock that this nation was founded upon starts to crumble.

Funny enough, the original NRA wasn't really concerned with civil liberties. The organization was formed around the time of the Civil War by Union Colonel William C. Church and General George Wingate in order to promote marksmanship, because, apparently, their troops couldn't shoot straight!

The NRA was granted a charter by the state of New York in 1871, and General Ambrose Burnside (also the founder of the sideburn) became the association's first president. Now led by Moses himself, Charlton Heston, today's NRA safeguards the Second Amendment, and also acts as a clearinghouse for information on gun safety, hunting, and sport shooting.

While you don't have to *carry chrome*—and frankly, we hope you don't— be psyched that you have someone to safeguard your right to do so.

REASON

89

WACKOS

In America, you have the freedom to be your own man (or woman), march to the beat of your own drum, even be a little nutty... particularly if you're rich. If you're a rich nutball, most folks call you eccentric.

We prefer the term "wackos."

From Anne Heche (and her alien alter-ego Celestia) to Jackie Stallone (and her psychic butt-print readings), we've got plenty of wackos. And hey, that's okay with us, because the shit they do sure is funny! Remember Vincent "the Chin" Gigante, the mob boss who walked the streets in his pajamas and bathrobe? How about when Prince wanted to be known by that ridiculous symbol? And that J. Edgar Hoover guy in a dress? He must've thrown some wild parties! Then there's H. Ross Perot, a self-admitted "crazy" who actually ran for President.

All exemplify the fact that Americans have the right to indulge in pretty much any ridiculousness they want, as long as they're not hurting anyone. And don't forget the American mantra: Any publicity is good publicity.

Even More American Wackos...

Marv Albert
Jim & Tammy Faye Bakker
Alec Baldwin
Ol' Dirty Bastard
Jerry Brown
Montgomery Burns
Mariah Carey
George Clinton
Bootsy Collins
Al Davis
Divine
Vincent "the Chin" Gigante
William Randolph Hearst
J. Edgar Hoover
Dennis Hopper
L. Ron Hubbard
La Toya Jackson
Angelina Jolie
Val Kilmer
Liberace
H. Ross Perot
Jimmy Piersal
Prince
Nancy Reagan
Dr. Laura Schlessinger
Marge Schott
Dr. Gene Scott
Al Sharpton
Jackie Stallone
George Steinbrenner
Barbra Streisand
Rip Taylor
Hunter S. Thompson
Billy Bob Thornton
Timmy
Donald Trump
Mike Tyson
Anybody who's been in *Cats*

Real American Wackos

HOWARD HUGHES

The patron saint of American wackos, Hughes started out reasonably sane and did a lot of cool stuff before the slippery slope of insanity (mixed with tons of dough) fucked his shit up. Before the wacko years, Hughes inherited Hughes Tool Company, then parlayed that into more bank when he founded Hughes Aircraft Corporation. He flew around the world in record-setting times, and controlled RKO Studios for a while. Around the 1950s all that stopped, and Hughes went into wacko mode: he lived as a recluse locked up in sealed-off hotel suites, tried to take over Las Vegas, reportedly drank his own urine, let his nails and hair grow to great lengths, and thought people were after him. Hell, people didn't even want to get near him!

MICHAEL JACKSON

If you believe the rumors, and hey, we do, Jacko is one odd fellow! The self-appointed "King of Pop" certainly has plenty to be proud of, including his early Jackson 5 stuff and albums like *Off the Wall* and *Thriller* (still the most popular record of all time). On the other hand, despite being African American, his current skin color is up to debate. While he denies multiple plastic surgeries, the fact that he now looks a great deal like Diana Ross has escaped no one. He tried to buy the Elephant Man's bones, and lives in a weird world of make-believe kingdoms, monkey friends, and little boys. His publicist might say he's making up for a lost childhood, but it's kinda creepy to us.

MARLON BRANDO

Brando burst on the scene with a crapload of attitude and a cool look that had audiences riveted. Then something snapped. During the filming of *Mutiny on the Bounty*, Brando was criticized for self-indulgence and huge tantrums. Francis Ford Coppola got him to chill out during the filming of *The Godfather* (though he mooned a group of extras during the wedding banquet scene), but he deteriorated during the painful filming of *Apocalypse Now*. Though he's done a few good flicks since then, all we can think of is that he kissed Larry King on the lips, weighs 300-plus pounds, wears several Rolexes at a time, lives on a remote tropical island, and, when he speaks, makes absolutely no sense at all.

ANDY WARHOL

We'll give props to Europe for Fauvism, Futurism, Cubism, Expression-ism, and Vorticism. But turning Campbell's soup cans into enduring icons of twentieth-century art? That's all us.

Andy Warhol is the father of one of our greatest artistic legacies: Pop Art. Born in Pittsburgh in 1928 to Czechoslovakian immigrant parents, he moved to New York and became a successful commercial artist. In the 1960s, he started painting pictures of soup cans, Marilyn Monroe, Coke bottles, and other everyday crap we hardly notice. On canvas, these banal images suddenly became strange, extraordinary strokes of pop culture genius . . . or something deep like that. After his buddy Robert Rauschen-berg taught him how to silkscreen, Warhol began mass-producing art like an assembly line (he called his studio "The Factory"), and made bank.

Warhol also made a film of a guy sleeping; produced the Velvet Under-ground's first record; started *Interview* magazine and threw some wild-ass parties, where people like Jim Morrison, Truman Capote, and Keith Haring got really wasted.

In 1968, he was shot by a crazy, pissed-off carpet-muncher. Some say he never fully recovered from the trauma. Warhol died in 1987, having snagged far more than his requisite fifteen minutes of fame.

Even More Great American Artists...

Ansel Adams
Diane Arbus
Jean-Michel Basquiat
George Wesley Bellows
Thomas Hart Benton
David Blythe
Harry Callahan
Mary Cassatt
Dale Chihuly
Chuck Close
Albie Cohen
John Singleton Copley
Ben Darby
Willem de Kooning
Richard Diebenkorn
Thomas Eakins
Walker Evans
Karen Finley
Eric Fischl
Leon Golub
Philip Guston
Keith Haring
David Hockney
Winslow Homer
Edward Hopper
Jasper Johns
Jeff Koons
Jacob Lawrence
Roy Lichtenstein
Sharon Lockhart

Other American Artists Who Rule!

GEORGIA O'KEEFFE

She's like the most famous female American painter ever. Born in a farmhouse in Wisconsin in 1887, Georgia knew by age thirteen that she wanted to be an artist. She studied art, taught art, and made art in a bunch of places, but ultimately called New Mexico home, where she painted canyons, sun-blanched cow skulls, and churches. But she's best remembered for her flowers, which look a helluva lot like a chick's privates—something Georgia never copped to. She also posed for naughty pictures for her avant-garde photographer husband. Georgia put down her paintbrush when her eyesight started failing in the 1970s, and died in 1986 at age 98.

JACKSON POLLOCK

One of the pioneers of Abstract Expressionism, Pollock was born in Wyoming in 1912, and later wound up in New York. In the late '40s, he developed his "drip and splash" style (think explosion in a spaghetti factory, Spin-Art, or vomit on canvas), which was supposedly a direct link to his unconscious. And apparently he had a lot of dark shit swirling around down there: he drank too much, was a social recluse, had mild learning and motor disabilities, was mean to his wife, and was generally self-destructive. But thanks to a big *Life* magazine article and art bigwig Peggy Guggenheim, he became America's first "art star." He died in a drunk driving accident in 1956, splattering his dashboard like one of his paintings.

ANNIE LEIBOVITZ

This renowned shutterbug has snapped pix of, well, everyone. That famous picture of naked John Lennon curled up with evil Yoko Ono? Annie took it hours before he was killed. The controversial *Vanity Fair* cover featuring a very pregnant Demi Moore? Annie. She's all about "posed spontaneity," using her lens to focus on hidden truths about her subjects. Born in Connecticut in 1949, Annie's been

Other American Artists Who Rule!

chief photographer for both *Rolling Stone* and *Vanity Fair,* and has shot award-winning ad campaigns for American Express and the Gap. What we dig about her is that her work is commercial without totally selling out. Plus, she still hangs with real artists. By the way, she's the first woman ever to be exhibited in the National Portrait Gallery in the Smithsonian.

Even More Great American Artists...

Robert Mapplethorpe

Robert Rauschenberg

Norman Rockwell

Ed Ruscha

John Singer Sargent

Cindy Sherman

Wayne Theibaud

Louise Tiffany

William Wegman

Benjamin West

James Whistler

Andrew Wyeth

FUN FACTS

American Graffiti

The word "graffiti" may be Italian, but the spray-painted street art style that it refers to is 100 percent American. Invented by the "bombers" and "crews" of New York City, graf's "wildstyle" lettering and colorful cartoon murals—as spectacular as any *legal* public art—were later exported to the walls, trains, and galleries of cities across the globe. Today, the Big Apple is still considered Mecca by graffiti artists all over the world.

**REASON
91**

CABLE

We live in the land of the free, a nation of boundless opportunity. We can choose to observe any religion we please; we can choose any career that suits us; and dammit, when we sit our ass on that couch, we can choose to watch any of a gazillion cable stations, all accessible at the flip of the remote.

Although Europe was the first to broadcast television via coaxial cable, we made the thing big and profitable. Formerly known as Community Antenna Television, or CATV, the first American cable systems were born in the late 1940s either in the mountains of Pennsylvania or Astoria, Oregon, depending on whom you ask. But your ability to channel-surf through a mind-numbing variety of programming came courtesy of Ted Turner, who in 1976 pioneered the notion of "superstation" broadcasting (TBS, CNN, TNT) to cable systems nationwide by means of satellite.

Today, out of the 102 million American homes with a TV, 70 percent have cable—and the option to tune into everything from the Cartoon Network to the History Channel. We've got stations devoted to family programming, smut, classic movies, and the weather; stations where you can laugh or cook or shop or watch wild endangered animals getting it on 24-7.

In the U.S. of A., you can ALWAYS find something cool to watch.

Cable Stations That Rule!

MTV

The first channel devoted entirely to pop music made its debut in 1981. MTV offered cutting-edge tunes to kids in big cities and po-dunk towns alike, setting off national trends like Flock of Seagulls hairdos and Madonna-style rubber-band bracelets. It made household names of bands like Winger; introduced kids in the 'burbs to boyz in the 'hood; and helped pioneer a slick, short-attention-span style of editing that had a profound impact on everything from movies to commercials. Today, MTV has over a billion viewers in 140 countries, making it the biggest single purveyor of pop and fashion on the planet. Some fans think it blows for moving away from its music video roots, but MTV still gets props for "Rock the Vote" and other campaigns aimed at raising youth consciousness.

THE FOOD NETWORK

Americans love TV and they love eating. It didn't take a genius to put the two together. We've enjoyed plenty of food-oriented shows over the years, but the Food Network takes the cake. Here you can learn how to make everything from egg salad to baby scallop ceviche. It's also home to Emeril Lagasse, the biggest chef/cooking teacher since Julia Child. To date, the Food Network has helped millions of Wolfgang Puck wannabes discern between arugula and frisee, and has opened millions more up to the many culinary opportunities afforded by pork fat. We're just waiting for that segment on pot brownies.

TV LAND & NICK AT NIGHT

Most countries have plenty of history books to document major events, revolutions, and cultural trends, but few (if any) have entire channels devoted to the preservation of classic TV. On cable stations like TV Land and Nickelodeon, folks like Mr. T, Ralph Kramden, Joe Friday, Maxwell Smart, The Beav, Jack Tripper, and the Brady family live on. Most Americans can't name all fifty states or all fortysomething Presidents, but thanks to stations like TV Land, they can tell you who said, "Marcia, Marcia, Marcia!" and "Sorry about that, Chief."

Even More American Cable Channels That Rule...

A&E
American Movie Classics
Animal Planet
Bravo
The Cartoon Network
Cinemax
Cable News Network
Comedy Central
The Discovery Network
E! Entertainment Television
Flix
Fox News Channel
Fox Sports
The Game Show Network
Headline News
The History Channel
Home Box Office
Independent Film Channel
The Learning Channel
The Movie Channel
National Geographic
Nickelodeon
PBS
The Playboy Channel
Public access
QVC
The Sci-Fi Channel
Showtime
The Spice Channel
STARZ!
Sundance
Turner Classic Movies
VH-1
USA Network

THE WWF

Imagine the cultural void that would be left without Hulk Hogan, The Rock, Stone Cold Steve Austin, the "figure-four leg-lock," and Wrestlemania.

Vince McMahon made wrestling what it is today: a rock 'n' roll soap opera of colorful characters who beat each other over the head with folding chairs. Wait a minute, hasn't wrestling always been like that? Oh yeah, he created the pay-per-view wrestling event, wrote great wrestling "plot lines," went public, and made bank!

Raised in a trailer park, Vince didn't meet his real father until he was twelve. But Dad, a small-time wrestling promoter, made up for his absence when he took Vince under his wing and showed him the ropes of the wrestling biz.

That's where the real story starts. Vince's big contributions didn't come until after he bought out Dad's wrestling league, the WWWF, and changed its name to the WWF. That one "W" made a huge difference! Vince retooled his events and switched his target audience from families and bluehairs to drunk men, transforming professional wrestling into the bone-crushing, body-slamming "sport" it is today. We won't comment on the disastrous XFL, but for the peerless WWF, thank you, Mr. McMahon!

American Pro Wrestlers Who Rule!

JESSE "THE BODY" VENTURA

Before being elected governor of Minnesota, Jesse Ventura was known to millions of wrestling fans as "the Body." Born Jesse Janos, he took the name Ventura after the coastal city of Ventura, California. He entered the famed square circle under the name "Surfer Jesse Ventura," but later switched monikers to "the Body" because Jesse—a former Navy SEAL—was also in great shape. Armed with his patented "Body Vise" finishing move, lotsa 'tude, and colorful attire, Jesse kicked a lot of ass during his WWF career. After his days in the ring were over, Ventura put his big mouth to good use as WWF's color commentator, while simultaneously appearing in movies like *The Running Man* and *Predator*. After serving a successful term as mayor of Brooklyn Park, Minnesota, Ventura was elected governor as the Reform Party candidate, beating Democrat Hubert Humphrey III and Republican Norm Coleman. Nobody claimed that this match was fixed.

THE ROCK

Born Dwayne Douglas Johnson, the Rock is a third-generation wrestler whose fame has far eclipsed that of both his father, Rocky Johnson, and his grandfather, High-Chief Peter Maivia. He "studied" at the University of Miami, but his real passion was football. Two ruptured disks in his back kept him from pursuing an NFL career, so he fell back on the family business. Since "winning" the Survivor Series in 1998, he's gone on to "win" countless other WWF titles, including the much-coveted World Heavyweight Champion belt. He's kicked everyone's ass in the ring, while his popularity is unrivaled. He wrote a best-selling book, and his appearance in *The Mummy Returns* set the stage for his starring role in *The Scorpion King*. *Can you smell what The Rock is cookin'?* It's called future earning potential.

Even More Wrestlers Who Rule...

ADRIAN ADONIS

ARN ANDERSON

KURT ANGLE

TONY ATLAS

STONE COLD STEVE AUSTIN

BRUTUS "THE BARBER" BEEFCAKE

CHRIS BENOIT

BIG BOSS MAN

NICK BOCKWINKEL

BRUISER BRODY

ROB VAN DAM

TED DIBIASE

JUNKYARD DOG

HACKSAW JIM DUGGAN

RIC FLAIR

TERRY FUNK

BILL GOLDBERG

SCOTT HALL

STAN HANSEN

BRET "THE HITMAN" HART

OWEN HART

MICHAEL HAYES

HILLBILLY JIM

HULK HOGAN

HONKY TONK MAN

CHRIS JERICHO

ROCKY JOHNSON

KANE

ANDY KAUFMAN

Even More Wrestlers Who Rule...

JERRY LAWLER

LEX LUGER

SHAWN MICHAELS

THE MISSING LINK

KEVIN NASH

PAUL ORNDORFF

DIAMOND DALLAS PAGE

KEN PATERA

THE PATRIOT

ROWDY RODDY PIPER

HARLEY RACE

DUSTY RHODES

JAKE "THE SNAKE" ROBERTS

BRUNO SAMMARTINO

RANDY "MACHO MAN" SAVAGE

SERGEANT SLAUGHTER

JIMMY "SUPERFLY" SNUKA

STING

BIG JOHN STUDD

TRIPLE H

THE ULTIMATE WARRIOR

THE UNDERTAKER

SID VICIOUS

FRITZ VON ERICH

KERRY VON ERICH

KEVIN VON ERICH

MR. WRESTLING II

BIG SHOW PAUL WRIGHT

American Pro Wrestlers Who Rule!

MICK FOLEY

Whether you know him as Cactus Jack, Mankind, Dude Love, or the best-selling author of *Have a Nice Day!*, odds are that you know this about him: Mick Foley's crazy! A smart kid from a nice middle-class family, young Foley invented the persona Dude Love, and proceeded to make backyard wrestling movies of himself diving off roofs until Dominic Deucci took him under his wing and trained him to do the stunts for "real" in the ring. Foley's wrestled for the CWA, WCCW, NWA, and WWF under different names, but he gained his greatest fame from his character Mankind (think Leatherface from *The Texas Chainsaw Massacre* with a sense of humor and a talking sock). Unlike some of his peers, Foley's brains were not turned to mush. He actually wrote his autobiography and a sequel on his own, getting good reviews and great sales. Foley came, he saw, he wrestled ... and lived to tell the tale, though he did lose a few teeth and a bit of his ear in the process.

PORN

Tera Patrick. Jenna Jameson. Midori. Janene. Asia Carrera. Nikki Tyler. Tori Wells. Ginger Lynn. Houston. Yup, we've got the best ass on the planet.

Best part is, in America, ass is quite accessible: in smut mags at 7-Eleven, strip clubs, online, by phone, and on DVD. The United States is the seat of the world's porn industry, racking up revenues of close to $6 billion yearly—that's a lot of Kleenex! The United States is where the bulk of the world's adult films are made, releasing 10,000 new titles in 1999 alone. L.A.'s San Fernando Valley is home to the world's largest community of porn stars (about 1,600), and fifty of the world's eighty-five top pornography companies.

This national resource isn't just comprised of women, either. Peter North, Ed Powers, Mr. Marcus, and Lexington Steele all qualify as the top-grade, USDA choice beefcake. Then there's Ron Jeremy—proof that in America, even gross fat pigs can get pussy.

TRASH

A chore reviled by children and husbands across the nation, taking out the garbage is absolutely no fun at all. But the next time you're dragging that stinky, bulging Hefty bag out to the trash bin, or dragging those cans out to the front of the house, thank your lucky American stars that you live in a country where someone is gonna pick that shit up.

America's management of trash is nothing to dump on. The U.S. sanitation system is one of the best in the world, annually lugging away 180 million tons of garbage so that you don't have to look at it, smell it, or contend with all the vermin and nasty diseases that propagate when it sits around piling up for weeks.

Also consider these facts: our toilets flush, our sewers work, we're tops in the world when it comes to recycling, and while it might not taste like Evian, U.S. tap water ain't ever gonna kill you.

More Great American "Trash"!

ANNA NICOLE SMITH

Bubbly Buxom Blonde Bags Billionaire! Hard work comes in all forms. In Anna's case, hard work means having big jugs, blonde hair, and the guts to marry a ninety-year-old billionaire, even in the face of criticism that you're a conniving gold digger. Born in Texas in 1967, Anna had dreams of becoming the next Marilyn Monroe. She appeared in *Playboy*, modeled for Guess! jeans and appeared in *Naked Gun 33⅓* before she found her true calling: marrying rich. In 1994, she tied the knot with oil tycoon Jay Howard Marshall. He "unexpectedly" croaked the next year, leaving the grieving widow with $450 million, and pissing off Howard's son. Lawsuits will be pending for some time. FYI: Anna's measurements are 39-27-39. Ouch!

THE JERRY SPRINGER SHOW

Shlock-TV host Jerry Springer has built an empire out of the exploitation of the trials, tribulations, and tempers of losers across America. Don't feel bad for them— they deserve it! Born in London in 1944, Jerry and family emigrated to New York when he was five. He got a law degree, worked for Senator Robert F. Kennedy, and was mayor of Cincinnati before he became an award-winning news anchor. Premiering in 1991, *The Jerry Springer Show* has become the nation's #1 daytime show, seen in over fifty countries. Are you a midget in a trailer park involved in a bizarre love triangle with your mom's boyfriend's daughter? Just call 1-888-321-5351. You could be Jerry's next guest!

OSCAR THE GROUCH

Big Bird's a dolt, Cookie Monster's a glutton, Kermit is always feeling sorry for himself, and Bert and Ernie have issues with their sexuality. But Oscar— *he's* someone we can relate to. Born on Sesame Street in 1969, this green, grime-loving furball reminds us that everyone has their shitty days, and that everyone's entitled to be a crank once in a while. He also reminds us that one man's trash is another's treasure. The ultimate cynic and social recluse, his passions include rainy days, anchovy milkshakes, and arguing for argument's sake. Interesting tidbit: Oscar was originally orange!

America, What's in Your Trash?

(A general overview of the country's garbage cans)

Paper products: 40.4%

Yard trimmings: 17.6%

Metals: 8.5%

Plastic stuff: 8%

Food scraps: 7.4%

Glass: 7%

Miscellaneous (rubber, textiles, wood, leather, etc.): 11.6%

Now, Here's What's in Our Trash!

(A detailed analysis of Rob's and David's garbage cans)

Empty Chinese food containers

Beer bottles

Jury summons

Beer cans

Two kinds of cheese

Hate mail

Old bread (blue and green)

Empty can, Glade

Sock with hole in it

Broken ax handle

Empty can, Dinty Moore Beef Stew

Promo copy, Mariah Carey's *Glitter*

First draft, *Why We Rule!*

Empty jar, pickled herring

FUN FACTS

Waste Not, Want Not

True, we produce a lot of garbage, but we also clean up after ourselves.

★ We're the top paper-recycling country in the world.

★ In 1999, America's recycling and composting activities prevented about 64 million tons of material from ending up in landfills and incinerators.

★ We recycle 28 percent of our waste, a rate that has almost doubled during the past fifteen years.

★ 42 percent of all paper, 40 percent of all plastic soft drink bottles, 55 percent of all aluminum beer and soft drink cans, 57 percent of all steel packaging, and 52 percent of all major appliances are now recycled.

★ Twenty years ago, only one curbside recycling program existed in the United States. By 1998, 9,000 curbside programs and 12,000 recyclable dropoff centers had sprouted up across the nation. As of 1999, 480 materials recovery facilities had been established to process the collected materials.

REASON
95

THE ATM

Americans cherish convenience almost as much as we covet freedom. Enter the automatic teller machine.

One day, while waiting in a long line at a Dallas bank, inventor Don Wetzel had an idea that would change history. Costing roughly $5 million to create, the first modern ATM was installed in a Chemical Bank in New York in 1973, and has gone on to become the way much of the world handles its daily banking needs. Quick cash, quick deposit, no annoying lines or tellers. You can even buy stamps!

Today, billions and billions of dollars in transactions are processed by hundreds of thousands of ATMs in virtually every country on the planet. More importantly, they're also located in virtually every strip club, casino, and bar.

★ **211** ★

Even More American Conveniences That Rule...

24-hour bail bonds

24-hour fitness

24-hour gas stations

24-hour drug delivery

Amazon.com

American Express

AM/PM minimarkets

Autozone.com

Caller ID

Call waiting

Car wash

Cell phones

Chinese delivery

Cup O'Pizza

Denny's

Directory assistance

Dishwashers

Domino's

Drive-thru dairies

Drive-thru liquor stores

Drive-thru wedding chapels

Escort services

Fluff-N-Fold

More American Conveniences That Rule!

7-ELEVEN

The name was originally meant to signify its hours of operation—7:00 A.M. to 11:00 P.M.—but today 7-Eleven is synonymous with around-the-clock convenience. Founded in Texas in 1927, 7-Eleven now serves over six million customers a day with over 5,700 stores worldwide. That's a crapload of cola Slurpies! Got the munchies and all the pizza places are closed? Thank heaven for 7-Eleven! You'll be downing hot dogs and nachos in no time flat! They're everywhere, and they're open 24/7 365 days a year, offering over 2,500 slightly overpriced products, including cold beer and condoms from friendly clerks who are there to help. Well ... everything but that last part.

MOTEL 6

They don't rent rooms by the hour, but they will leave the light on for ya! Hitting the road and need a cheap, clean place to stay? Look no further than the great Motel 6 chain. With over 129 lodges to their name, you can drive all around this country of ours and find a clean place at a reasonable price to spend the night. Their spokesman, Tom Bodett, has become an American icon on his own, dishing out homespun wisdom on his "We'll Leave the Light on for You" commercials, one of the longest-running ad campaigns in history. Here's something you might not know: When he's not busy pitching the 6, Bodett is a writer and commentator on National Public Radio.

KINKO'S

Americans do business twenty-four hours a day. Whether you gotta put together a professional presentation or you're printing concert flyers for your crappy death metal band, Kinko's is there to help you get the job done right ... or at least quickly. Founded thirty years ago as a small copy hut next to a taco stand in Isla Vista, California (right near the UC Santa Barbara campus), Kinko's now

More American Conveniences That Rule!

has over 1,100 branches around the world. Featuring tons of copiers, computers, and binding services, it really is America's home office. Pretty much the only things you can't copy at Kinko's are money, the complete works of Stephen King, and your hairy ass.

SIT & SPIN

Don't you hate doing laundry? Wouldn't you rather go drink beers, listen to music, grab some grub, and hang out with friends? Well, in America, you can do all of that at the same time. Just as we pioneered conveniences like the drive-thru, the Internet, and the ATM, our entrepreneurial minds have come up with a place where you can wash a load of whites and get loaded at the very same time. Seattle's Sit & Spin is a laundromat, club, and restaurant all in one, featuring a full bar, live bands, food ranging from sandwiches to Pesto Rotini . . . and a fleet of washers and dryers. Other interesting places to do the laundry include the Brain Wash Café & Laundromat in San Francisco, and Suds & Duds in New York and Carrboro, North Carolina. Talk about good clean fun!

Even More American Conveniences That Rule...

Food delivery

Freeways

Goober's PB & J Mix

Home Depot

Hospitals

The Internet

Liquor delivery

Mapquest.com

Microwave ovens

Minute Rice

OnStar

Operators standing by

Plumbing

Porta Pottis

Remote control everything

Room service

Roto-Rooter

Supermarkets

Tijuana

Traveler's checks

TV dinners

Western Union

UPS

Your daily newspaper

ELBOW ROOM

When it comes to real estate, we got a lot of it. 3,537,440 square miles, to be exact, and 3,794,085 square miles if you count our bodies of water.

We started out with a measly thirteen colonies, and in just over two hundred years we've grown into the world's third-largest country, jam-packed with a veritable crapload of natural resources, climates, and topographies: Alaska's glaciers, Florida's eighty-degree winters, Hawaii's rain forests, and Nebraska's, um, open space. From the mountains to the prairies to the oceans white with foam, we got it all, baby!

SUCH A DEAL!

*America bought Alaska from Russia
in 1867 for $7.2 million. About thirty years later,
gold was discovered in Alaska, followed by oil.
Once considered Seward's Folly, it's now
thought of as the best land deal in history.*

FUN FACTS

The Brightest Place on the Planet . . .

Yuma, Arizona, is the sunniest place on the planet, with an average annual 4,127 hours of sunshine. Phoenix is a close second.

STARBUCKS

There used to be a time when you couldn't get a decent cup of joe in this town. But now, thanks to Starbucks, you can enjoy your favorite "gourmet" brewed beverage (cappuccino, espresso, Frappuccino) at any time of the day in any city . . . in any mall . . . on every street corner.

Starbucks first opened for business in 1971 at Pike Place Market in Seattle. More of a coffee shop than the phenom we know today, it was Howard Schultz who convinced the company to try a new concept: the coffee bar! The original seventeen-store chain has since grown into a coffee empire of over 3,300 locations worldwide, leaving the likes of Maxwell House and other less gourmet brands in the dust.

Starbucks democratized the gourmet coffee house, making it easy to be a finicky snob when it came to your morning brew, whether you're knocking back a Doppio Espresso or a half-decaf, half-caf non-fat soy grande latte.

THE
INTERNET

Who logged on first?

In 1962, MIT's J. C. R. Licklider conceived of a "Galactic Network," a globally connected set of computers through which everyone could check out data from any site. Meanwhile, it was the height of the Cold War, and folks at American think tank the Rand Corporation needed a way for U.S. authorities to chat with each other in the aftermath of a nuclear attack. Rand's Paul Baran came up with a communications network that was set up like a fishnet, so that info could find its own path through the network even if one section was destroyed. Baran's meditations led to a small network connecting computers at four university campuses around the United States, and the seeds of the net were sown.

Today, over 400 million people around the world—130 million in America alone—use the net to buy movie tickets, send cutesy e-mails, and download bootlegged Metallica tunes and naked pictures of Bonnie Raitt (LOL). By 2005, a billion people will be connected globally. BTW, we have more users and Internet service providers than anyone else. ;-)

American Web Sites That Rule!

Even More American Websites That Rule...

aintitcoolnews.com
allmusic.com
alternet.org
ampland.com
atomfilms.com
amateuravenue.com
backyardwrestling.com
blogdex.media.mit.edu
bullseyeart.com
cbssportline.com
carmen-electra-naked-and-
shannon-elizabeth-nude.com
dooce.com
disinfo.com
drudgereport.com
etiquetteforoutlaws.com
fark.com
fuckedcompany.com
google.com
heavy.com
hitsmagazine.com
hiphop-elements.com
ifilm.com
imdb.com
ironminds.com
mapquest.com
memepool.com
neumu.com
nomayo.com
obscurestore.com
pitchforkmedia.com
rhymer.com
romp.com
rotten.com
rottentomatoes.com
sleazycolin.com
spiritcam.com
themorningnews.org
thesmokinggun.com
televisionwithoutpity.com
trashy.com
tsn.com
upcomingmovies.com
virtualcrack.com
whywerule.com
zefrank.com

EBAY

The world's largest online flea market was founded in 1995 by Pierre Omidyar of San Jose, California. Today, with 29.7 million registered users and $5 billion in gross annual sales, it's the most popular shopping site on the net. Log on, and sell or bid on anything—a slightly dented tuba, a 1998 Acura, good karma, even a lock of Elvis's pubic hair, complete with certificate of authentication. Just about the only thing you can't trade are live organs, illicit drugs, and small children. Not only has this site facilitated the exchange of "tchotchkes" across the globe, but it also acts as an online "bluebook," letting you know just how much some schlub will pay for your own discarded junk.

JUMPTHESHARK.COM

Named after the Fonz's famous dare to "jump the shark" in the California episode of *Happy Days*—the episode that marked the popular TV series' decline—this unique site chronicles the exact point in time when great shows turn to gimmicks to save their sorry-ass ratings. Categories include "Same Character—Different Actor," "Death," "Singing," "I Do," "A Very Special..." and others. Our favorite JTS category, though, is "Ted McGinley." Says the Shark: "Chances are that if Ted is anywhere near your cast, consider the show on the downward spiral." *Happy Days, Welcome Back Kotter, The John Larroquette Show,* and *Married with Children* all swirled around the bowl once he showed up. Fans of *The West Wing* and *The Practice* should take note of recent Ted sightings.

RATNIGHT.NET

After you finish surfing through the entire contents of the Library of Congress, reading all of Proust's *Remembrance of Things Past*, and watching *The Godfather* for the fortieth time, check out Ratnight.net as a way to chill out your taxed brain with a snootful of stupidity. A favorite of ours, it just goes to show that any schmuck with a web site idea, an html program, and too much time on his hands can take a drunken idea and turn it into a globally available drunken idea. Here's the site's premise: get a giant rubber rat and stick him in as many unlikely places as possible: a Las Vegas casino, the wilderness, art museums, atop the Golden Gate Bridge, and between countless sets of buxom breasts. The site also includes movies of the rat in a strip club, having sex with a hot dominatrix, starting bar brawls, and meeting a terrible fate that we won't disclose here.

WE HELP

Here and abroad, when disaster strikes—flood, famine, earthquakes, whatever—you can count on Americans to lend a helping hand.

There are American charities to help with everything: food, clothing, medicine, cash, or other forms of assistance. In 2000 alone, Americans ponied up over $200 BILLION to more than 125,000 different charities as varied as the American Red Cross (who help everyone), World Vision (starving children in Africa), and the Nature Conservancy (helps with land conservation). Meanwhile, our government donated around $6.8 billion to help out overseas.

We have a lot; we give a lot.

On the other hand, we do apologize for rotund Sally Strothers's pitches for "Feed the Children." Having a spokesperson who looks like she just ate a bag full of Big Macs hanging out with emaciated little kids just doesn't work for us.

MAN'S BEST FRIEND

We have a soft spot for the mutt. It's the perfect metaphor for a nation of crossbreeds like ourselves. The dog is also an American symbol of companionship, courage, and loyalty, from the fireman's dalmatian to Lassie, Old Yeller, Clifford, and Snoopy. We've got a whopping 58,500,000 pooches—twice as many as any other nation.

Some countries let 'em roam in wild, rabid packs. Others stir-fry them with bamboo shoots. But here, the dog is truly man's best friend. We take our canines hiking, play Frisbee with them, use them to protect our homes, and bring them to the dog park as an excuse to meet dates. We pamper 'em with gourmet dog food, doggy salons, and professional dog walkers, while organizations like the ASPCA, the Humane Society, and a gazillion pet rescue and adoption groups keep 'em safe, happy, and off the streets.

In addition to being the world's biggest dog lovers, Americans can also claim credit for fake dog poo, the Pooper Scooper, Snoop Dogg, Lil' Bow Wow, "Atomic Dog," and "Stupid Pet Tricks."

FUN FACTS

Pussy Galore!

In addition to having the most dogs in the world, America is tops when it comes to cats. In 1999, our feline population was around 73,000,000. The favorite American name for kitties? Tigger, followed by Tiger, Smokey, Shadow, and Sam.

REASON

101

FRIVOLITY

There's no denying it—we play hard. We also lounge hard.

Every year, Americans watch 408,800,000,000 hours of TV, spend over $7,500,000,000 at the box office, and shell out $34,500,000,000 for toys. Every day, we wallow in not-so-essential decisions as Gucci or Prada; soy or nonfat; highlights or lowlights; face masks or face peels; Overnight or 2nd Day; MTV-1 or MTV-2; Backstreet or *NSYNC; shaved or waxed; paper or plastic; tastes great or less filling. We read *The Globe*, *Stuff*, and *Muscle & Fitness*, and our minds are occupied with not-so-burning questions like which star is boffing which, who will get voted off the island ... and a million other things most of the world doesn't have time to obsess about.

Are we frivolous? Hell, yeah! And we deserve to be. After a sixty-hour work week spent coming up with ideas and inventions exported to all corners of the earth—no midday siestas, no six-week vacations—we've earned the right to indulge in some frivolous pleasures, dammit!

Every year, more people visit our country than any other. Why? Because we're fun. America is the world's preeminent purveyor of pop culture, and everyone wants to come to the party. The best part is, everyone's invited; there's no guest list.

Why We Suck!

With freedom comes the responsibility to own up to our misdeeds, foibles, and other stupid bullshit. As Americans, we deeply apologize for the following...

Carrot Top	Recounts	Sam Donaldson's toupee
Pauly Shore	Care Bears	Anti-pot laws
The Pax Network	Wine in a Box	Scientology
The macarena	The Moral Majority	Fanny packs
Rosie O'Donnell	Americans abroad	The *Lambada* movies
Rosie magazine	Jerry Falwell	1-800-COLLECT commercials
Obesity	Jimmy Buffett	VH-1 Divas concerts
Watergate	The Manhattan Transfer	Network television movies
Banner ads	Mannheim Steamroller	Largest defense budget
Jaywalking tickets	Shoulder pads	50-minute hour
Meter maids	Lite beer	Nagasaki
Countless frivolous lawsuits	Tofurkey	Joseph McCarthy
Olestra	The leisure suit	Jenny McCarthy

Exxon Valdes

JonBenet Ramsey

Largest jail population

Gary Condit

Emmanuel Lewis

3,700 people on death row

Schoolyard shootings

Gang bangers

Homelessness

13,000 murders a year

Hate crimes

ATM surcharges

Susan Smith

New Jersey Turnpike

The IRS

Too much suing

Miracle Whip

Ambrosia salad

Bob Dornan

David Duke

Just say "no"

Pollution

Biggest energy hogs

White boys trying to be down

Temptation Island

Tony Little

Aaron Carter

Rocky Mountain oysters

Mountain Dew

Celebrities singing the
   national anthem

Jazzercise

Infomercials

Telemarketers

American tourists

Americans speaking French

Did we mention lite beer?

That stupid singing bass

Kenneth Starr

The Beadazzler

Macramé

Weekend craft fairs

Ice Capades

Vietnam

Japanese internment camps

"Separate but equal"

Rules

The KKK

Robert Bly

Enron

Oliver North

Gay-bashing

Anti-semitism

SlimFast

Kenny G

Kenny G's hairstylist

Tanning salons

Lee press-on nails

Dental dams

Steven Seagal

Chuck E. Cheese

Kathie Lee Gifford

Jar Jar Binks

"Please hold, an operator
   will be with you shortly"

Our treatment of
   Native Americans

16,000 sexual harassment
   lawsuits a year

Timothy McVeigh

Linda Tripp

Slavery

Parking tickets

The 80-hour workweek

Jesse Helms

Jesse Jackson

Sally Jessy Raphael

O-Town

Crazy Town

White zinfandel

98 Degrees

DMV lines

O. J. Simpson

All of O.J.'s friends

Last call

SOURCES

BOOKS CONSULTED:

Bowser, Eileen. *The Transformation of Cinema, Volume 2 1907-1915*. California: The University Of California Press, 1990.

Cohen, Carol, editor. *Benét's Reader's Encyclopedia, Third Edition*. New York, New York: Harper & Row, 1987.

Cohen, Rob & Wollock, David. *Etiquette for Outlaws*. New York, New York: HarperCollins, 2000.

The Columbia Dictionary of Quotations is licensed from Columbia University Press. Copyright © 1993, 1995 by Columbia University Press. All rights reserved.

Crystal, David, Editor. *The Cambridge Factfinder, Fourth Edition*. Cambridge, UK: Cambridge University Press, 2000.

Encarta® 98 Desk Encyclopedia © 1996-97 Microsoft Corporation. All rights reserved.

Epstein, Dan. *Twentieth-Century Pop Culture*. London, UK: Carlton Books Limited, 1999.

Footman, Tim, Editor. *Guinness World Records 2001*. New York, New York: Bantam Books, 2001.

Gregory, Hugh. *A Century of Pop: A Hundred Years of Music That Changed the World*. Chicago, Illinois: A Cappella Books, 1998.

Jones, Judy & Wilson, William. *An Incomplete Education*. New York, New York: Ballantine Books, 1987.

Magill, Frank N., Editor. *Great Women Writers*. New York, New York: Henry Holt and Company, 1994.

McGeveran, William A., Jr., editorial director. *The World Almanac and Book of Facts 2002*. New York, New York: World Almanac Books, 2002.

Mussuer, Charles. *The Emergence of Cinema, The American Screen to 1907*. California: The University Of California Press, 1990.

Panati, Charles. *Panati's Extraordinary Origins of Everyday Things*. New York, New York: Harper & Row, 1987.

Romanowski, Patricia & George-Warren, Holly, editors. *The New Rolling Stone Encyclopedia of Rock & Roll*. New York, New York: Fireside, 1995.

Shindler, Merrill. *American Dish: 100 Recipes from Ten Delicious Decades*. Santa Monica, California: Angel City Press, 1996.

Spignesi, Stephen J. *The Odd Index*. New York, New York: Plume, 1994.

———. *The U.S.A. Book of Lists: The Ultimate Compendium of All Things American*. Franklin Lakes, New Jersey: The Career Press, Inc., 2001.

Trager, James. *The People's Chronology*. New York, New York: Henry Holt and Company, 1994.

———. *The Women's Chronology*. New York, New York: Henry Holt and Company, 1994.

Wallechinsky, David & Wallace, Amy. *The Book of Lists*. New York, New York: Little Brown & Company, 1993.

Webster's Dictionary of American Authors. New York, New York: Smithmark Publishers, 1996.

The World Almanac® and Book of Facts 1997 is licensed from K-III Reference Corporation. Copyright © 1996 by K-III Reference Corporation. All rights reserved.

WEB SITES CONSULTED:

Askjeeves.com

Cia.gov/cia/publications/factbook/geos/us.html

CNN.com

Fortune.com

Grolier.com

Google.com

Ideafinder.com

MLB.com

NFL.com

Nalc.org

NBA.com

Nps.gov

Rollingstone.com

Supremecourthistory.com

TheOnion.com

Thinkquest.org

Top-biography.com

Usahistory.com

Whitehouse.gov

Wic.org

Yahoo.com

Zerowasteamerica.org

Numerous other company web sites

PHOTO CREDITS:

Courtesy the authors: pp. 3 bottom; 7 middle; 8 top and bottom; 22; 31 bottom; 37; 54; 57; 61 bottom; 63 middle; 70; 90; 96; 97 top, middle, and bottom; 103; 108 top; 111 middle; 119; 120 top, middle, and bottom; 121 top; 137; 147 bottom; 154 top, middle, and bottom; 156; 158; 159 top; 168 top and bottom; 170 bottom; 173 middle and bottom; 190; 202; 212 top, middle, and bottom; 216

Courtesy Getty Images: pp. 11 top, middle, and bottom; 17; 19 bottom; 25; 26; 33; 35 top and bottom; 38; 39 bottom; 42 top, middle, and bottom; 43 top, middle, and bottom; 44 top and middle; 45 top and bottom; 46; 47; 48; 50; 53; 55 middle; 58; 62; 63 top and bottom; 67; 68 top and middle; 69 top and bottom; 72; 74; 77 top, middle, and bottom; 78 top, middle, and bottom; 79 top, middle, and bottom; 80 top, middle, and bottom; 81 top and middle; 82 top and bottom; 83 middle and bottom; 84; 87; 93; 94; 95 top, middle, and bottom; 99 middle; 100 top, middle, and bottom; 101 top; 104; 105 top, middle, and bottom; 106 top, middle, and bottom; 107 top, middle, and bottom; 108 bottom; 109 top, middle, and bottom; 110 top, middle, and bottom; 111 top and bottom; 112; 113; 114; 115 top, middle, and bottom; 116; 118; 121 middle; 123; 128; 129 top, middle, and bottom; 131 top and bottom; 132; 138; 140; 142 top, middle, and bottom; 145 top and bottom; 148; 153; 159 bottom; 160; 162 top, middle, and bottom; 163 top, middle, and bottom; 165 bottom; 166; 167; 168 middle; 170 top and middle; 172; 178; 188; 191 top, middle, and bottom; 193; 196; 198 top, middle, and bottom; 199; 200 top, middle, and bottom; 203 middle and bottom; 204; 205 top and bottom; 206; 209 top and bottom; 211; 214

Anthony Neste HBO/Courtesy Getty Images: p. 99 top

Buena Vista Television/Courtesy Getty Images: p. 102

The Jerry Springer Show/Courtesy Getty Images: p. 209 middle

NBC/Courtesy of Getty Images: p. 81 bottom

Twentieth Century Fox/Courtesy Getty Images: p. 56

Universal International Television/Courtesy Getty Images: p. 99 bottom

Courtesy Digital Playground: pp.135 top, middle, and bottom; 136 top, middle, and bottom; 207

Courtesy Doug Brooker: p. 44 bottom

Courtesy Easy B: pp. 150; 194

Courtesy Ron Popeil: p. 146 top

Courtesy Kate Romero: p. 23 top

Courtesy Trudy: p. 220

Courtesy Mary, Bridget, and Trashy Lingerie: p. 134